What Others Are Saying . . .

"In *The Bush Always Burns*, Heath Adamson has written a book for anyone who wants to know a different Jesus than the one you may currently know or grew up hearing about. Heath wants you to intimately know the true Jesus you can really trust with life's unannounced moments. Throughout the book, he offers encouraging examples of courageous people who stood in the gap (that place of weakness, vulnerability, and danger) for him and others (Heath calls them "rainmakers") to introduce him to God and His power. I highly recommend this debut work from an author we're sure to hear more about."

Wilfredo "Choco" De Jesús, senior pastor, New Life Covenant Church, Chicago, IL; author of *In the Gap* and *Amazing Faith*

"In *The Bush Always Burns*, Heath Adamson shows us a Jesus who, like Moses, is waiting for us to turn and see the burning bush in front of us and the sacred ground directly beneath us. He is a Jesus who longs to rewrite our stories. I'm thankful Heath is sharing his inspirational story while waking us up to the realities of heaven. I encourage all leaders to read these words of wisdom and learned insight."

Dr. George O. Wood, general superintendent, The General Council of the Assemblies of God

"The world, indeed the church, is desperate for leaders like Heath who are authentic, vulnerable, and saturated with the pursuit of Christ, because truly abiding in Him is the only way to walk in the Spirit and find peace in the storms that invariably rise against us in this life. Heath's tender heart beckons us all to see what he has seen—to *taste and see that the Lord is good.* Using crisp writing and utterly relatable stories from his own life, Heath leads us all into a deeper understanding of what it really means to *know* Jesus."

Ted Dekker, *New York Times* best-selling author of over thirty novels

"Heath Adamson is a choice servant of God. The best way I know to describe my respect for him is to borrow the description God used to describe His servant Caleb: *"my servant Caleb has a different spirit and follows me wholeheartedly"* (NIV). That's how I view Heath. He's an exceptional friend, thinker, leader, and servant of God. In his book *The Bush Always Burns* you'll quickly discover what I mean. As he shares his personal faith journey, you'll be encouraged to evaluate your own and challenged to see God's divine hand at work in the most ordinary moments of life."

Scotty Gibbons, national youth ministries strategist, The Assemblies of God National Leadership and Resource Center

"To know who we are, we must know the true Jesus. I love what Heath says in this new book about how our identity is directly connected to who Jesus is. He is a Jesus who loves and pursues us. We just have to turn and see the bush burning in front of us before we can see ourselves as sons and daughters of God. The message Heath brings through *The Bush Always Burns* is so needed in today's culture."

Scott Wilson, senior pastor, The Oaks Fellowship; author of *Ready. Set. Grow: 3 Conversations That Will Bring Lasting Growth to Your Church*

"Heath Adamson is one of those young pastors with a story—a good story you want to read. But more important than his life's story is how he points to God as the One who rewrote it. Heath reminds us that God is in the business of rewriting stories, especially for people who think they're too far away for God to ever reach them. Young pastors can learn from Heath's story and the examples he offers of how God longs for and leads us into a deeper awareness of and intimacy with Him."

Justin Lathrop, founder, Youngpastors.com

"The first time I heard Heath Adamson speak, he said, 'I never want to forget what it's like to be lost.' The way he talked about the gospel engaged my mind and moved my heart to greater consideration of the goodness and grace of Jesus. *The Bush Always Burns* is timely, needed, compelling, and well worth your time. Heath's stories will not only capture your attention and imagination—they will also help illustrate deep spiritual truths. In this book, you are reading words written by a man who models what he teaches and inspires others to do the same. Heath is a leader I would follow into any situation and a friend who helps me better see and appreciate the Father, the Son, and the Spirit."

David Hertweck, district youth director,
New York Youth Ministries, Assemblies of God

The Bush Always Burns

Jesus in the Unannounced Moments of Life

HEATH ADAMSON

vital-resources.com

Copyright © 2015 by Heath Adamson
ALL RIGHTS RESERVED

Published by Vital Resources
1445 N. Boonville Ave.
Springfield, Missouri 65802

No part of this book may be reproduced, stored in a retrieval system, or transmitted in any form or by any means—electronic, mechanical, photocopy, recording, or, otherwise—without prior written permission of the publisher, except for brief quotations used in connection with reviews in magazines or newspapers.

Cover design by PlainJoe Studios (www.plainjoestudios.com)
Interior design by Prodigy Pixel (www.prodigypixel.com)

Unless otherwise specified, all Scripture quotations are taken from the Holy Bible, New International Version®, NIV®. Copyright © 1973, 1978, 1984, 2011 by Biblica, Inc. ™ Used by permission of Zondervan. All rights reserved worldwide.www. zondervan.com. The "NIV" and "New International Version" are trademarks registered in the United States Patent and Trademark Office by Biblica, Inc.™

Scriptures marked The Message are from The Message: The Bible in Contemporary Language®. Copyright ©1999 by NavPress. Used by permission. All rights reserved.

Scriptures marked (ESV) are from the ESV® Bible (The Holy Bible, English Standard Version®), copyright © 2001 by Crossway, a publishing ministry of Good News Publishers. Used by permission. All rights reserved.

Scripture quotations marked (NLT) are taken from the Holy Bible, New Living Translation, copyright © 1996, 2004, 2007 by Tyndale House Foundation. Used by permission of Tyndale House Publishers, Inc., Carol Stream, Illinois 60188. All rights reserved.

The Original Aramaic New Testament in Plain English with Psalms & Proverbs; Copyright © 2007; 8th edition Copyright © 2013. All rights reserved. Used by Permission.

NOTE: Some of the names in this book, as well as some identifying details, have been changed to protect the anonymity of the people involved.

ISBN: 978-1-68066-000-5

Printed in the United States of America
18 17 16 15 • 1 2 3 4

Dedication

To Ali, for slowing down long enough to notice, and for
rewriting the story for generations to come with Jesus and me.
I cherish you and thank you for allowing me to walk with you
on His path.

Contents

Foreword		*1*
Introduction		*7*
CHAPTER 1	*What It Feels Like to Be Lost*	*21*
CHAPTER 2	*Searching for Something*	*39*
CHAPTER 3	*Paving Our Way to Jesus*	*55*
CHAPTER 4	*Rainmakers*	*71*
CHAPTER 5	*It Matters What You Call Yourself*	*81*
CHAPTER 6	*How Close Is Close Enough?*	*103*
CHAPTER 7	*Questions About God*	*115*
CHAPTER 8	*Four Sleepless Nights*	*133*
CHAPTER 9	*Don't Act Like a Christian*	*149*
CHAPTER 10	*Complicating the Simple*	*169*
Endnotes		*187*
Acknowledgements		*191*
About the Author		*193*

Foreword

W ithin minutes of first meeting Heath, one word echoed through my spirit: *authentic*. And then two more: *true believer*.

Now, when I say true believer, I don't mean someone who believes that Jesus is the Son of God, because even the demons know this and it profits them nothing. Rather, I mean one who believes *in* Jesus rather than merely believing anything *about* Him. One who puts their trust *in* Jesus rather than in all the mechanisms of this world.

The world, indeed the church, is desperate for leaders like Heath who are authentic, vulnerable, and saturated with the pursuit of Christ because, truly, abiding in Him is the only way to walk in the Spirit and to find peace in the storms that invariably rise against us in this life. Heath's tender heart beckons us all to see what he has seen—to *taste and see that the Lord is good.*

Using crisp writing and utterly relatable stories from his own life, the author leads us into a deeper understanding of what it really means to know Jesus. As he writes: *"Sometimes, what we think we know about Jesus prevents us from knowing Him,"* because knowing in the biblical sense is a deeply intimate union between two and has little to do with knowing *about* something.

Like the child Jesus beckons us to become, Heath has tasted and he has seen. He knows his Father.

And knowing goes further, because unless you truly know your Father, you cannot truly know who you are. Why? Because, as Heath writes: *"Satan's original lie says that God is not who He says He is, and you are not who He says you are."*

Do you really know who you are? Not what others say you are based on this doctrine or that doctrine? Have you truly come to know yourself as the child of your Father?

There's really only one way to know yourself, Heath writes. *"We'll never know who we are or why we matter until we meet Jesus. Our identity is in Christ. When we meet Jesus, we discover who we are."*

Maybe you once knew who you were, but have forgotten. You're a Christian, but have you *met* Jesus recently? Have you known Him today? Is your faith in Him, or is it in all the troubles and worries that seem to threaten you in this life? Faith in Him offers peace in the storm; faith in the world offers fear. Where is your faith?

If you're like many Christians, you may not be sure. And this is where *The Bush Always Burns* begins—with some frank and honest reflections that we all know but are afraid to talk about. To quote Heath: *"Have we become more concerned with following Christianity than with following Jesus? Are we awake— really awake—to the realities of Jesus?"*

Fantastic questions. And they resonate with me deeply, even though my background might be the polar opposite of Heath's. As you'll read in his own words, he grew up knowing far more about the occult than Jesus or Christianity.

I, on the other hand, grew up as the son of missionaries who left everything in the West to take the good news to a tribe of cannibals in Indonesia.

Nevertheless, although I grew up in the church and was very familiar with all of its doctrine, I never really knew who I was or why I was significant. As such, on one level or another, I spent most of my life feeling inferior, rejected, even abandoned. I could never quite live up to the expectations other people had of me. As a result, I felt insignificant.

In fact, I see now that my entire life has been one long search for my identity and for significance in *this* life though I was secure in the next life.

As I grew older and troubles came my way, many of the neat answers I had memorized in church seemed to fail me, sometimes quite spectacularly. I began to see cracks in what had once seemed so simple to me.

I was supposed to have special power to bring healing and turn the other cheek and refrain from gossip and not judge. I was supposed to be a shining example, known by the world for extravagant love, grace, and power in all respects. And yet, while I heard the rhetoric of others, I didn't seem to have these powers myself.

During my teens, I was sure that it was uniquely my fault—I didn't have enough faith, I needed to try harder and do better. Others seemed to have it all together, but I was a failure.

Can you relate?

Then I began to notice that everyone seemed to be in the same boat, beginning with those I knew best. When my relationships failed; when disease came close to home; when friends turned on me; when I struggled to fit in; when life sucked me dry, I began to wonder where all the power to live life more abundantly had gone. Then I began to question whether or not it had ever really been there in the first place. Maybe that's why I couldn't measure up.

So I pressed in harder in the hope of discovering God's unconditional love. I went to Evangel University; I was filled with the Spirit and spoke in other tongues and even saw people healed on occasion.

But deep down inside, I still couldn't seem to measure up.

And when I couldn't measure up, I began to see with perfect clarity that most who claimed to live holy lives were just like me—a fact that was apparent to everyone but them. Did not *Yeshua* teach that jealousy, gossip, anxiousness, and fear are just another kind of depravity? Did He not say that even to be angry with someone or call him a fool is the same as murder—not just kind of/sort of, but really?

So then, I seemed to attend a church of murderers every Sunday and Wednesday. I asked myself, *How, then, does one find and know peace and power in this life when surrounded by such a great cloud of witnesses who only pretend to be clean by whitewashing their reputations while pointing fingers of judgment?*

And I wasn't alone. All of my friends were asking the same questions.

So many Christians today see a system that seems to have failed them. They have found the promises from their childhood to be suspect if not empty.

What about you? You're saved in the next life as a matter of sound doctrine, but do you often feel powerless and lost in *this* life?

Later in my life, I began to truly know my Father and truly believe in Jesus and as a result know myself because I was in Him and He in me. He is *the bush that always burns*, and I walk on that holy ground, in the world but not of it.

So simple yet so profound! That knowing—that tasting of my true identity—was like a fireworks show going off in my heart and mind and soul. I was loved! I was my Father's child and I knew Him.

"This is eternal life," Jesus said, "to *know* the Father." And eternity is now, unbound by time. This is abundant life.

This knowing is the difference between walking on the troubled seas of your life and drowning in them. Whenever I forget who He is and who I am in Him, I can feel myself drowning.

If you find yourself struggling to know your Father and yourself in Jesus, then Heath offers a beautiful word for you today: "*Despite your searching, Jesus is near. The bush is burning, even in the midst of your raging storms.*" What is that burning bush? God's presence, right here, right now, regardless of where you are. "*Any time we become profoundly aware of His presence,*" Heath writes, "*we are changed. In the presence of love, we understand.*"

So then, read what Heath has written; listen to the Spirit if you have ears to hear. Taste and see that the Lord is good. What a beautiful, beautiful gift Heath offers in *The Bush Always Burns*.

Ted Dekker, *New York Times* bestselling author
of over thirty novels

Introduction

=====================================

Have we become more concerned with following Christianity than with following Jesus?

F orty years is a long time. Quiet desperation. The desert is a deadly place to be when you're hanging on for one more breath but can barely express it through words. Though Moses couldn't have known it, God's providence was at work in this barren place to free him. According to a podcast I heard from W. A. Criswell years ago, "If Moses had ascended to the throne of the Pharaohs, we would have known the hallowed leader as just another Egyptian mummy in a museum. If he hadn't been forced to flee from the Pharaoh's palace and his lifestyle of affluence, Moses would have been the iron fist, forcing the Hebrews to live as slaves."[1]

In many ways, I know that same providence. It rescued me from slavery of a different form.

Quiet desperation haunts many of us, and it's lethal. Moses traversed the burning sands of the Sinai Peninsula, a parched throat his companion, and sat down by a well. He was weary and wondered why his life had played out so discouragingly. This wasn't how it was supposed to end. Too much had happened in his favor. As an infant, he had survived the Egyptian Pharaoh's massacre of Hebrew boys and through a series of divine events was handed off to the Pharaoh's daughter, becoming the son of an Egyptian princess. In a nation where four hundred years of slavery was the norm, Moses spent each day in affluence and wealth. Not surprisingly, God eventually chose him to create the blueprints for the tabernacle. God wastes nothing in His sovereign plan.

Now, because of other events in his life—which I'll discuss in more detail later—he's in the desert. The location is symbolic. Here, Moses is isolated, afraid, and embarrassed, feeling like he may have missed God's calling altogether. A leader groomed to rule on a throne has evolved into a caretaker of sheep in the middle of nowhere.

Sometimes, like Moses, we find ourselves in the middle of nowhere, but that's exactly where we're supposed to be. History calls them the unannounced days—those ordinary moments in our lives that aren't scripted or heralded by angelic voices. In hindsight, when we look back at our lives, we often realize that these unannounced moments were actually critical turning points, when life shifted. Yet when we were walking through those days, we were unaware.

Moses was unaware. As Criswell continued to speak about Exodus 3, he said, "In the Sinai Peninsula, the sun rose over the eastern horizon as always, the wind sifted the sand in his hair, and the shadow of the mountain peered down upon the has-been ruler."[2] The sheep scavenged for herbage. As in all the previous days, the well would once again provide hydration and relief from the heat. This had been his routine for forty years. In this barren place, Moses could no longer hear the cries of Egypt's injustices. He sat in tangible silence.

But here, he could know God. Here, God could finally get through to him. The forty years in the desert weren't a waste; God used Moses's quiet desperation to help him "unlearn" the eloquence of royalty as He prepared his heart for an even greater kingdom.

Nothing's Ordinary

The staff in Moses' hand would serve as a reminder that under the watchful eye of the Creator nothing is ordinary. W. A. Criswell discussed the destiny of Moses' staff—that one day it would stretch out over the Red Sea and part the waters. The staff would stretch out again, and the waters would come back together, drowning Egypt's army (Ex. 14:16, 21–27). The same staff would hit the rock at Mount Horeb, and water would pour out (Ex. 17:5–6), and then later it would oversee a dynamic victory over the Amalekites (Ex. 17:11).[3]

Whether it's a shepherd's staff, a loaf of barley bread that tramples the tents of the Midianites (Judg. 7:13 14), or a young boy's sack lunch in the hands of Jesus, nothing is ordinary when God is there. Likewise, no person is ordinary. When we fall prey to believing we're ordinary, we become enslaved to striving for achievement and significance. I know this well. Growing up, I felt ordinary, common, overlooked, and easily absorbed into my surroundings. In my life, there was no Mount Horeb but another mountain called hopeless. Like Moses, day after day I wandered around in a destitute existence with just enough relief to start another day. God had something better for my life. He has something better for your life too. That's why Jesus came.

Waking Up the Church

One hundred miles is a short distance. To our knowledge, Jesus never traveled more than one hundred miles from His hometown, yet His ministry spread to all corners of the earth. Jesus was in Caesarea Philippi, of all places, when He first described something called the church, a community where conversation was to be valued more than achievement, miracles were disguised as interruptions, and love was embodied. Church was to be a laboratory where dreams were born and hope was restored.

Think about it. Rather than a belief system, a building, or a political lens with which to view reality, Jesus ascended to heaven leaving only this: the church. A cause motivated by justice. A conversation to continue. A community whose shadows would creep upon the earth as love turned the black-and-white world of religion into a colorful masterpiece. The community known as the church should be the very manifestation of Jesus.

Dreams can become stagnant over time, and ideas can atrophy. After two thousand years of Christ's church upon the earth, we are in the midst of a moment when the landscape of Christian faith may appear barren. Similar to the barren moments in Moses' time, the hope of many feels elusive. The church has resources, services, leadership, and organization, which in and of themselves, can be good assets. However, apart from the divine voice, they are hollow. It's good, then, from time to time, to revisit why we do what we do and who Jesus really is in our lives.

Sometimes even in the center of good things, we need to turn aside and see who He truly is, which begs the question: Have we become more concerned with following *Christianity* than with following Jesus?

If we're moral and dutiful but *asleep* to the realities of heaven, we'll miss seeing the God who is at work right in front of us. We'll miss the unannounced days. If we criticize culture rather than engage in it to bring about positive change, we'll lose out on the opportunity to participate in the kingdom. Jesus didn't come to criticize culture but to create it. He searched for those who were steeped in moral exercise but numb to the present kingdom. The great God was within reach, and yet many were unaware, quietly desperate. Jesus came to give them sight to see the present kingdom. He does the same today.

Turn and See

Exodus 3 brings us back to Moses, still living in the desert in quiet desperation. But this day—this unannounced moment— will signal the end of these uneventful, mundane forty years.

Here's the thing: The desert is where God shows up.

On this day, in this seemingly forsaken place, God showed up for Moses—not just in an audible voice, which would have certainly been enough to catch Moses' attention. On this day, Moses saw the burning bush. In Exodus 3:3 Moses says, "I will now turn aside and *see* this great sight, why the bush does not burn" (ESV, emphasis mine). Can you imagine? A bush is on fire, and yet the branches aren't even singed. If that doesn't get your attention, I don't know what will!

The first and most obvious response to this passage is something to the effect of, "Wow! God performed such incredible miracles in the Bible!" You might even think to yourself something like *I wonder why He doesn't perform miracles like that anymore.* But if this is the extent of our understanding of this passage, we're missing something important.

When we look a bit deeper, we see that the Hebrew word Moses used for "see" is *ra'ah,* meaning "to perceive." The Greek version of this word is *horao,* which means "revelation." I've heard many rabbis comment on this passage, pointing out that the bush had been on fire before Moses recognized it, but Moses finally perceived it that day. It wasn't that he *saw,* with his eyes, something new God was doing. It was that he "saw" (perceived, had a revelation about) something God had been doing all along.

Don't miss that. The bush had been burning all along— for centuries, in fact. *The bush always burns, and the ground is always sacred.*

I wonder how many others walked by the burning bush, unaware. I wonder how many times we wander in our personal deserts, feeling sorry for ourselves or afraid or ashamed— unaware of the divine things happening all around us. What if we could wake up to the realities of heaven like Moses did? While Scripture outlines the boundaries of what revelation looks like, what if we had our own revelation?

I like what theological ethicist H. Richard Niebuhr says, "The greatest Christian revolutions come not by the discovery of something that was not known before. They happen when somebody takes radically to something that was already there."[4] This is what happened for Moses, and I think this is what can happen for us, if we're willing and ready to turn and see that the bush is always burning and the ground is always sacred.

Turn and see. It sounds simple enough, and it is. But sometimes we have a way of taking what is simple and making it complicated.

To be honest, I've done my fair share of complicating the simple. By the time I was a junior in high school, I was steeped in the occult, abusing crystal meth and LSD, and regularly traveling the spiritual realms. My life felt scary and dry, and I was desperate for someone to show me the way. Like Moses, I was in a spiritual desert, desperate for the tiniest sign that God was real, all the while ignoring the divinity of God all around me.

The bush always burns, and the ground is always sacred. The question is: Are we willing to *turn* and *see?*

The Puzzle Pieces of Faith

When I was young, one of my favorite places to visit was my grandmother's house. Saturday mornings, as the tradition went, I would go over to Ma's house (as I called her), and she would pour me a glass of ice cold Coke. I was always amazed at how she could fit just a *few* more drops into my Styrofoam cup without it ever spilling over. It seemed like magic.

Along with our Coke, she would open a package of oatmeal cookies—you know the kind: the hard ones with that thin layer of icing on top, similar to the texture of Elmer's glue. We would sit around and eat cookies and drink cold Coke, or hot coffee. The cookies didn't taste good, but they didn't have to. They were the perfect accompaniment to my beverage of choice. And in the first grade, treats like this seemed perfect.

Ma was obsessed with Scrabble and puzzles. After breakfast, we would take her to Dahl's Foods, and she would meander up and down the aisles looking for cat food to feed the stray cats in the neighborhood. The list was the same every time—Purina cat food, the infamous oatmeal cookies, Coke, deviled ham, and every now and then she'd splurge on a melon.

Ma selected her melons with a religiosity you've never seen before. She would pick up the melon, spank it numerous times, and shake it. Then she'd hold it up to her ear and listen. To this day, I'm not sure what she learned when she held that melon up to her ear, but she always seemed concerned about getting the right one.

After returning from the store, we would unload the groceries, do some yard work, and then venture into the house for our Coke, deviled ham sandwiches, and cookies. We rarely sat at the kitchen table for our treats. That was the place where Ma did her puzzles, and puzzles trumped family meal-time any day.

For weeks, Ma would labor intensely, putting together a jigsaw puzzle (she always bought the big ones with 6,648 pieces) only to finish and throw it away. Then, inevitably, she would pick up another one on our monthly trip to Dahl's. I always noticed her routine with a new puzzle: She removed the cellophane, took the lid off, and flipped out the puzzle pieces right side up with the color staring at the ceiling. Then she propped the lid of the box against the wall and proceeded to find the four corners. "Branded by Milton Bradley" was always in the upper right-hand corner . . . a freebie.

Once the four corners were in place, Ma began to build the puzzle, finding the straight-edged pieces first. She completed the frame and started to fill in the pieces at every appropriate spot— all based on the picture on the puzzle lid.

That lid was her compass. Every action was prescribed by and tethered to the picture on the lid. "Don't you dare put that piece of goldenrod there," the lid seemed to say. "You need a turquoise piece instead."

As a child I remember thinking, *What would happen if I switched the lid?* I wondered if she could even continue her puzzle building without the correct compass in place. Of course, one day, my wondering led me to test my theory—which led to one of only two times in my life when Ma spanked me. It's amazing how hard a grandma can hit when you mess with her puzzles. (And don't be fooled by her age. That woman had a pretty good arm on her. Must have been from all that time spanking melons!)

I can't say I blame her. Especially now, looking back, I can see how difficult it would be to build a puzzle from the wrong picture. All the pieces you think should be there aren't. All the pieces you have don't seem to match the image in front of you. Everything is confused. Everything seems upside down. Nothing makes sense.

Thinking about my grandmother with her confused puzzle makes me wonder about you and me. How many of us are building our faith off of a confused picture, a switched image? Think about it for a minute. What "picture" are you using to guide your spiritual life? Are you looking to the Bible? To the church? To the people around you? Perhaps you've never even thought about it.

Are we building our lives from the picture of Jesus or the picture of Christianity?

When we build from the wrong image, it doesn't matter what we do to get a piece to fit. We can pray long and hard about it, be disciplined, fast, read Scripture, basically do all the right stuff, but no amount of wrestling will make a piece fit in a place where the Creator never intended for it to fit. When we have all of the right pieces—prayer, fasting, good behavior, an outward and strong stance against culture, spiritual discipline, and access to the Scriptures—but we're building from a different lid—we can kill Jesus. Seriously. Jesus was killed by those who had all the right pieces, but whose lid was switched.

Who we imagine Jesus to be is critical.

If you look to the people around you as your guide, the "lid" to your puzzle, then you'll miss it. You'll miss Him. Many of us already have. We're building our lives off of an image that never has been and never can be the image of God. Scripture makes it clear that we are made in His image, but He alone is the true reflection. When we look to our right and to our left to see a picture of God, we get confused.

If we're building our faith from the wrong picture, no wonder we're confused. No wonder things just don't seem quite right. We have the right pieces, but we're building from the wrong lid. The pieces we have don't seem to fit. If we're going to re-create the picture we're looking at, we need elements and images that don't seem to exist in our pile of puzzle pieces. No wonder we're frustrated. No wonder the "Christian life" seems so impossible to live. No wonder so many are "rejecting" Jesus. But maybe they're not rejecting Jesus so much as they're rejecting the brand of Jesus we're selling them.

The Power of Profound Knowing

What does it mean to *know* Jesus? There are many different kinds of "knowing." We can know something in our minds—the way we do when we read about it in a book or somebody tells us about it. We can know through intuition or memory, a less concrete but still valuable way of knowing. Or we can know something through experience—not because we've read about it, necessarily. Not because anyone has told us it's true. But because we have lived, breathed, and experienced it for ourselves.

This is the kind of "knowing" the Bible says happens between a husband and wife when they are united together as one. It's the kind of knowing that happens over time, when you've walked next to someone and have seen that person up close. Marriage is the ultimate "up close" kind of relationship. No wonder Scripture uses the word "know" when it talks about the marriage relationship.

Do you *know* Jesus? Do you know Him in the intimate way a husband and wife know each other? Have you moved beyond pleasantries and niceties to get to the real stuff?

Nobody ever told me about Jesus. I didn't go to church on a regular basis. But when I met Him face to face in my bedroom one night, that moment changed me. I knew Him. I couldn't stay asleep anymore. And if there's one thing I've learned about walking with God, it's this: Once you know Jesus—really *know* Him—the fruit that comes from knowing Him is inevitable.

I'm no different or better than anyone else in the church today. In fact, if I read you my "résumé," so to speak, you would probably cringe. I would rank among the social outcasts Jesus dared to hang out with. I've done things, gone places, and experimented in ways you've probably only read about in books or seen in movies. I'm aware of my need for grace and redemption. I'm thankful for mercy.

If there's one thing I learned early on in my life—even in the midst of experiences with witchcraft and the occult—it's this: Spiritual realities are happening, whether we choose to acknowledge them or not. The bush is always burning, and the ground is always sacred. God is real, regardless of our response to Him. Whether or not we experience those realities is up to us. Do we have a keen awareness? Are we willing to "turn and see"?

Jesus is who He says He is, but not necessarily who we perceive Him to be. He is holy. He is all-powerful and has conquered sin and death. He is our Creator and our Redeemer. He is the one true God. He speaks in the desert. If we can wake up to this reality, if we can be in tune with it, if we can add to our old ways of knowing a new way of knowing Jesus, then we will find the passion and love that God always intended for us. The bush is always burning, and the ground is always sacred. We simply need to turn and see.

Do you want that? Do you want to see God move in our generation, and in our nation, in a way we've never seen Him move before? Do you want to see miracles happen? Do you believe all of that is possible? I do, but the only way it's possible is if we wake up to the realities of His presence—even when they are unannounced—His power and His redemptive work all around us.

All is not lost. We don't need to destroy and start again. We're not worshipping the wrong God. We just need a new awareness of who He is and how He is moving. It's not a matter of a hidden truth we must reveal; rather, it's a matter of slowing down long enough to notice what is easily overlooked. When we can cultivate that, as a community, there will be *no stopping* the movement of a God who flows from that place. The gates of heaven will open. His grace will pour out. Get ready. The unannounced moments are coming.

.

CHAPTER ONE

What It Feels Like to Be Lost

What does "lostness" look like in your life?

I know what it feels like to be lost—deep into drugs and the occult. I was using Ouija boards, studying witchcraft, and getting drunk on a regular basis. If that sounds crazy to you—if it intrigues you or seems difficult to comprehend—hang with me. The most dangerous thing we can be is lost without knowing we are lost.

Imagine for a minute you're driving through an unfamiliar city without a map or GPS. You know your destination, but you don't necessarily know the way to get there. You might think you know where you're going, but there comes a point when you realize—you're lost. You don't recognize any of the landmarks. You don't see any street names you know. It can be frustrating to travel long and far only to realize you've gone nowhere.

Now picture someone sitting in your passenger seat. Perhaps it's a friend or a spouse or a companion who's traveling with you. As you navigate, you don't say anything to your passenger. You just keep driving. Is your passenger any less lost than you are? Of course not. You're both in the exact same predicament. It's just that one of you is keenly aware that you are lost while the other is not. The truth of the matter is that we can be lost without knowing we're lost; and until we admit how lost we are, we'll never find our way.

Moses was lost for forty years without realizing how lost he was. He wandered the desert, traveling hundreds of miles. In fact, the "lost" years of Moses' life were actually quite productive. He started a family, launched a career, and made a home. He had a steady job as a shepherd, supported his wife and kids, and did the best he could to be a good man. Imagine how devastating it must have felt for Moses to realize that all the work he had accomplished during those years—all the creativity and innovation, everything he had built—was for nothing. Forty years is a long time to be lost.

Maybe the idea of being lost doesn't resonate with you. Or maybe that word sinks deep and you think, *yes—lost. I haven't wanted to say it, but that's what I am.* Either way, Moses is a prime example of how we can be lost and not realize it. We can think we're progressing quite nicely while being completely lost. And yet Moses is also a prime example to us of how—no matter where we're standing, no matter our circumstances or our landscape— the ground is always sacred. The bush is always burning.

Good Guy, Bad Guy

For most of us, the mere mention of the name Judas causes an almost physical reaction. "Judas" has become a cultural term, synonymous with backstabber, double-crosser, spy, traitor, or weasel. He was one of the twelve disciples, but for the most part we don't think of him that way. We think of him as one of the "bad guys," one of the primary people who handed Jesus over to the Romans to be killed. Next time you think of Judas, however, consider this: He was actually a pretty good guy.

Judas walked with Jesus. He was one of Jesus' chosen few. He learned from Jesus and was attentive to Him. Judas was a good, upstanding citizen. Jesus trusted him enough to put him in charge of managing the money for the disciples; not just a little bit of money—a lot of money. Judas didn't wake up one day and decide to betray Jesus. For months, perhaps years, betrayal brewed inside him before he ever followed through. No one around him would necessarily have noticed his internal condition. He might not even have noticed it himself. It was a slow fade. He was the epitome of lost without knowing he was lost.

Although I'm grateful for the many exceptions to this statement, if I could pick anybody in the Bible to describe what I see when I look at the modern church, and at times even my own life, I would pick Judas. A lot of people talk about Peter as the symbol of today's church because He denied Christ after seeing all of the Messiah's miracles. But I think Judas is the picture of today's church. Peter was afraid of his surroundings and cowered in fear. Judas blended in well with Jesus on the outside, but inwardly he was far away from the Lord's heart.

The bush was burning right around him—right in front of him, in fact—but he didn't seem to notice. The ground he walked on was sacred (it was literally the same ground Jesus walked on), but that didn't change Judas's ultimate demise or faulty decision. It's amazing how we can share experiences with God, even be in His presence, and walk away untouched if our hearts are not open to Him.

Judas was close to Jesus—close enough to Jesus to dip His bread into the cup (a custom designed to put a guest of honor on display). Yet, at some point, Lucifer found a friend in Judas, who became an integral part of the plot to murder Jesus. Luke 22:3 says, "Then Satan entered Judas, called Iscariot, one of the Twelve." That seems crazy to me. Satan *entered* Judas—a man who was at Jesus' side during His entire public ministry?

So how did Judas end up betraying Jesus? I would argue it's the same way any of us end up at that place—step by step . . . little by little. We don't make big decisions to jump off the deep end. We make small decisions to ignore or resist. The bush is ablaze right beside us, but we choose not to turn and see it. The ground is sacred right beneath us, but we choose not to acknowledge it. There was no "major moment" when Judas decided to betray Jesus, just subtle moments when Judas decided to ignore the glory of Jesus and seek his own glory.

Matthew 26:20–23 reads, "When it was evening, he reclined at the table with the twelve. And as they were eating, he said, 'Truly, I say to you, one of you will betray me.' And they were very sorrowful and began to say to him one after another, 'Is it I, Lord?' He answered, 'He who has dipped his hand in the dish with me will betray me'" (ESV). The passage goes on to say, "Judas, who would betray him, answered, 'Is it I, *Rabbi?*'" (ESV).

Don't miss the subtlety here. In that tiny moment, we get a glimpse into the mind of Judas. Jesus was the rabbi in Judas' life, not his Lord. The Scriptures say that every knee will bow and every tongue confess—not that Jesus is Savior, or rabbi (although He is both those things)—but that He is Lord.

From an outsider's perspective, Judas must have looked like all the other disciples. He was sitting at the table with them, doing all the same things they did. But in his heart, he saw Jesus as a "good teacher" rather than as "Lord."

Judas' behavior should be a stern warning to each of us. This is what happens when you're close to Jesus but

> Just because you feel like you're in the middle of nowhere doesn't mean you're lost.

He isn't your Lord. When Jesus is simply a "good teacher," when He's the reason you have a good life—great job, kind spouse, kids in private school—but you don't fall down at His feet and worship Him, the inevitable end is betrayal. The bush is burning, and the ground is sacred, but you're missing it.

Also, note this: Judas didn't betray Jesus for an incredible sum of money. He did it for thirty pieces of silver—the price of a common slave. To Judas, it wasn't about financial gain; it was about power and prestige, about making a name for himself.

Ultimately, the end for Judas was suicide. In some ways, you might expect this to be true. Certainly, he must have felt profound guilt over murdering Jesus. But Judas' obvious depression and eventual suicide make me wonder: If he was so miserable, how did he miss the joy, peace, and love to be found in Jesus? How did he go for so long without finding his way when the Way was right in front of him?

Just because you feel like you're in the middle of nowhere doesn't mean you're lost. Joseph was in solitude and darkness in Pharaoh's dungeon, but he was far from lost. An abducted victim named Daniel was taken by force to a foreign land—but it wasn't foreign to God. John the Baptist found himself living in the middle of the desert, in complete isolation, but he wasn't lost at all. Being lost doesn't necessarily look the way we think it does.

In Romans 13:11, Paul says, "Awaken from your slumber!" A person who asks a probing question is not lost.

This is one of the other confusing aspects of being lost. You might feel stuck where you are. You might feel like you're in the desert. You might wonder what you're supposed to do next. You might have some probing questions. You might feel like you've been waiting for years, or even decades, for God to fulfill His promises for you. But take heart. The fact that you feel lost is, strangely, an indicator that you're not as lost as you think you are. Turn and see. Look underneath you. The bush always burns, and the ground is always sacred.

We can be lost and not know we're lost. We can feel lost and not actually be lost. This is confusing, I know, but the point is this: When we admit we're lost, God always helps us find our way. Not always in the way we might imagine, or in the time, but the ground beneath us is always sacred. The bush is always burning.

When I was lost, I tried everything to find my way. I was frantic in my searching, desperate. In many ways, this desperation is what led me down the paths of drugs and séances. These were destructive to my life, but I'm not sure they were any more destructive than the paths Judas walked—which must have looked like church attendance and a 401k and kids going to a great college. No matter what version of lost we live, it never ceases to be dangerous and painful.

What does being lost look like in your life? Maybe for you, it's drugs or alcohol, like it was for me. Perhaps it's simply trying to keep up appearances . . . good grades . . . career success . . . accolades and awards. Who would have thought that being a "good person" could get in the way of a life with Jesus? Either way, the answer Jesus gives is simple but not always easy. Directly underneath you—and all around you—are the divine answers you've been waiting for. The bush always burns, and the ground is always sacred.

At the end of the day, do you call Jesus "good teacher" or Lord?

Our Need for Jesus

One of the most important things to note about Judas—and to learn from him—is that he didn't understand his need for Jesus. As far as Judas knew, he didn't need *anything*. He had everything under control.

By our standards today, we might say he had a good job, a savings account, was trusted by his companions, and had a 401k and two great kids who never got into trouble. He had a good education, a beautiful wife who respected him, and a happy marriage. But despite having all the blessings of God, Judas didn't really *know* God. He hadn't experienced Him.

His reputation ran wide, but his character wasn't deep. His leadership abilities were flawless, but he forgot how to serve. He networked well but was inwardly alone. He enjoyed life on the stage in front of the masses who followed after Jesus but, unfortunately, he traded the altar for that stage. His prayers were prayer-less, and his hefty offering was shallow.

Judas was lost, but he didn't know it. He was in an environment rife with the movement of God, yet he remained oblivious. When we come to God desiring something specific—a great marriage, a new car, a job, entrance to a specific college—we might get what we want, but we run the risk of leaving satisfied, feeling like now we have all we need. When we come to God looking simply for God Himself, we begin to realize all we could ever want is found in Him—not the things He offers. "Seek first his Kingdom and his righteousness," says Matthew, "and all these things will be given to you as well" (6:33).

Jesus teaches this lesson in a profound and unmistakable way in the Gospels, when He drives the money changers out of the temple. Interestingly enough, Matthew, Mark, and Luke record Jesus driving money changers out of the temple at the *end* of His three-year ministry. But in John's account, He does it at the beginning. The details of the two accounts are different enough that we can see these events were actually two separate occurrences. In other words, Jesus sandwiched His public ministry with two displays of His intolerance for the abuse of truth. Leave it to Jesus to both come in and go out with a bang.

The disciples saw everything that took place. Jesus used a homemade whip of ropes and loosed the animals. Clanging coins echoed as they hit the ground. Money boxes cracked as He turned over tables, His voice thundered, "Take these things away; do not make my Father's house a house of trade" (John 2:16, ESV). Stunned onlookers would have recognized this as a reference to Psalm 69:9, "Zeal for your house has consumed me and the reproaches of those who reproach you have fallen on me" (ESV).

Like Judas, the money changers in the temple were standing on sacred ground, yet they couldn't have been more oblivious. The power and presence of God—the person of Jesus—was right in their midst, yet they missed it. They ignored the glory of God for the purpose of their personal gain.

Not long ago, I was with a friend in Jerusalem, and we got to spend some time with a history buff. We spent most of our time at historical sites. He took us beneath the streets in Jerusalem, where we walked through the unearthed ruins of a former priest who took up residence in first-century Jerusalem. We walked around the foundations of a first-century house and while we did, our friend gave us the history—one fraught with greed, posturing, positioning, and networking.

He explained how there was power, affluence, and influence to be found in the "system" of the priesthood, which meant some were motivated to keep the system functioning properly no matter what. Power and influence can be an intoxicating force. As our guide talked, I couldn't help but think how dangerous it is to have influence, power, or resources supported by a system—even if the system is religious or based on an appearance of good.

In some ways, it's unavoidable, but my prayer is that we never worship the system over the God who ultimately called us to it.

At one point, our friend explained that the Sadducees (a sect of leaders in the priestly caste) purchased the system from the Romans. This meant the temple tax had to be paid with a Tyre coin, made of pure silver, and the priests controlled the prices of the tax. It also meant the sacrificial system was more of an economic engine than it was an opportunity for people to have an encounter with the divine. In fact, many people couldn't afford to give sacrifices at all. Some priests starved to death because greedy/crooked priests wouldn't share revenues.

> People wanted what God could give them, but they didn't want God Himself.

Standing below ground in Jerusalem, hearing this, I felt the tears rise behind my eyelids. How in the world could they—could we—forget God who was the reason for it all? How could we become so lost without knowing it? And if it's possible to be so lost without realizing it, is it possible I'm this lost? Is it possible you are? It's a sobering thought to consider we're all just one step away from depravity—clothed in power, wealth, and influence.

No wonder Jesus was so angry. Yes, there were some who came to buy sacrifices with pure hearts. But even those pure intentions were muddied by the injustice and corrupt hearts of the leaders. Almost everybody there was lost. Very few realized the ground they walked on was sacred. None of them was in tune with the realities of heaven unfolding around them.

In the few words Jesus said to the crowd, He distinguished between "my Father's house" and a marketplace. "My Father's house" alludes to a place or encounter where being with, treasuring, and honoring God in service and holiness is priority; a place where it's precious simply to be with God (Psalm 84:10). Yet the focus on God had been replaced in this setting by a system—a system that was leading (some intentionally and others unintentionally) to destruction and despair.

Jesus, who "knew what was in man" (John 2:25, ESV), saw beyond the religious system and directly into the hearts of the money changers. Hearts where a love for position, power, and religion were prevalent and sincere love for God was absent. People wanted what God could give them, but they didn't want God Himself. Many of them looked for God but didn't find Him. Others weren't even looking anymore.

Can you relate?

Albert Einstein once said, "Perfection of means, and confusion of goals seem to characterize our age."[1] I think this means that many of us are lost and we don't know it. We're following the rules. We're good, upstanding citizens, like Judas. We get good grades and do our homework and go on to have great careers and decent marriages and pay our bills. But we have lost our way—even though the Way is right in front of us. We have everything we need, so we don't understand our need for Jesus.

Revelation 3:17—the passage that describes what it means to be a lukewarm Christian—reads, "You say, 'I am rich; I have acquired wealth and do not need a thing.' But you do not realize that you are wretched, pitiful, poor, blind and naked."

Wow! In other words, the most wretched thing you can possibly do, the thing that will cause God to spit you out of His mouth, is to forget you need Him. You think you're rich, but you're pitiful and naked—incredibly sobering.

In Mark 7:9, Jesus says to the scribes and Pharisees, "You have a fine way of rejecting the commandment of God in order to establish your tradition!" (ESV) They had allowed the "system" they established as a roadmap to God to *replace* God Himself. I don't know about you, but for me, this sounds painfully familiar. Can you see ways in our culture—or in our lives—where we've allowed the system we built as a way to God to replace the Way?

The scene in the temple that day wasn't an isolated instance of questionable worship. It was the outward manifestation of greed, cloaked with religion: "This people honors me with their lips, but their heart is far from me; in vain do they worship me" (Matt. 15:8–9, ESV). The pattern, unfortunately, has repeated itself throughout history. God is perpetually in our midst, yet we don't see or acknowledge Him.

Do you know how desperately you need Jesus? I can honestly say I do, but that understanding hasn't been easily won. Not many would wish for my testimony. Like I've said, I've been to some really dark places in my life—places where no one should choose to venture. I've been lost. Sometimes we have to admit we're lost before we can be found.

Dark Places

The truth is, if we slow down long enough to remember, we've all been to some dark places. Sometimes we find ourselves in dark places not because of our choices but the choices of others. Sometimes we're the driver. Other times, we're the passenger. Sometimes we can see how lost we are. Other times we don't realize it until we've missed our destination by a long ways. In the end, we have no one to blame for where we end up. We can't control everything that happens to us, but we can control how we respond.

The choices of others filled my childhood with fear and sadness. I learned at a young age about broken trust and broken promises. As a child, the night terrors were so bad I spent days in doctors' offices as they tried to discover what was wrong. No one was ever able to point to the exact problem. Spiritual problems can't be solved with an earthly consciousness.

I saw the ravages of sin in my childhood. I saw what anger can do to someone and how bitterness rots to the very core. I learned from those closest to me how to converse with the spiritual realm. I remember talking with demons and watching candles float off of tables and chairs scoot across the basement floor. No wonder the night terrors were so bad.

My access to alcohol was far from whimsical, and experimentation with hallucination fed my curiosity for the world beyond. By the time I entered middle school, I had most everybody around me fooled. Because I was a good student, in the accelerated classes, in programs such as "talented and gifted" and "conflict managers," and was a decent athlete, no one fully understood my darkness. I was popular and dressed nicely, but inwardly I was dead. I was lost and nobody knew it. Darkness doesn't always look so dark, especially when it's cleaned up and made to look nice.

It reminds me of what Jesus said in Matthew 23:27, "Woe to you, teachers of the law and Pharisees, you hypocrites! You are like whitewashed tombs, which look beautiful on the outside but on the inside are full of the bones of the dead and everything unclean." Speaking of dark places, Jesus compares the Pharisees—some of the most religiously and culturally upstanding people of His day—to tombs, where they kept dead bodies.

> If we want to get to the place where we truly grasp how much we need Jesus, we have to be willing to admit the darkness in our own hearts.

The significance of this is huge. Tombs or sepulchers were above-the-ground edifices to house bones/cadavers. A committed teacher of the law or common Hebrew would have fled from these "unclean" tombs. The tombs were whitewashed for at least two reasons. First, the paint alerted someone that the tomb was nearby—so they could avoid contact. Second, it was a beautification and preservation technique. A whitewashed tomb looked more beautiful than just a regular one.

This was me—a whitewashed tomb—all cleaned up on the outside and extremely good at covering up the death beneath the surface.

I've been to dark places, which is why I'm certain where I would be without Jesus. No matter the circumstances of my life, I know—completely and deeply—how desperately I need Him. I pray regularly that the grace of God will be present in my life so I never forget where I've been. Are you keenly aware of the dark places in your heart? We all have them. We're all lost. Are you willing to see and admit how lost you truly are? This is the first step toward your personal discovery of the bushes burning in your life.

The danger of not knowing our personal darkness is huge. We run the risk of finding comfort in our spiritual pedigree—upbringing, obedience, or church attendance—rather than in Jesus. Beware of the belief that you're exactly where you perceive yourself to be. Jesus addresses this with one of the most provocative verses in all of the New Testament: "See to it, then, that the light within you is not darkness" (Luke 11:35). It's a travesty to walk around in darkness and discover that we had only *imagined* our path was illuminated. Darkness knows no bounds. We're all born separated from God.

If we want to get to the place where we truly grasp how much we need Jesus, we have to be willing to admit the darkness in our own hearts. We have to be willing to abandon the "system" we think will get us to Jesus—the rules, religion, and outward appearances of goodness. We have to know that we're lost and know that Jesus is the Way—the *only* way—home.

Where Is Jesus in All of This?

Is it really possible to lose sight of Jesus even though He's part of our daily religious rhythm? The answer is yes. The Old Testament and the New Testament testify to this. Ezekiel 10 tells how the glory of the Lord departed from the temple, and for approximately one hundred years, the Israelites continued to gather and go about their routine. First Samuel records the life of

King Saul who, when the Spirit departed from him, continued to hold a place of earthly leadership—though in heaven his position was forfeited.

Luke 2 tells how Jesus' parents went to the temple for the dedication of their twelve-year-old son, as was the custom. After leaving the temple to sojourn home, Joseph and Mary discovered they didn't know where Jesus was. Aside from the obvious parental panic of losing a child, have you ever thought how ironic it was that Jesus was lost, of all places, during a religious ceremony and in a religious community?

Even though it appears Jesus is with us in our religious practices, we would do well to avoid the assumption that we are actually with Him. It's entirely possible to lose Him in the midst of trying to find Him or at least our version of Him. In the midst of custom and culture, sometimes we miss Him. The bush is always burning, and the ground is always sacred—but that doesn't mean you recognize it. You can stand among a group of people who call themselves Christians and still wonder *where is Jesus in all of this?*

Far beyond the witchcraft I was involved with or the drug abuse that trapped me for years, the darkest place I've traveled may very well have been those days when I thought I was close to Jesus but then discovered my heart was hard. Take a minute and look into your own heart. Is there any trace of darkness there? Do you know what it feels like to be lost?

Many have asked Jesus to be the Savior of their souls. Many have committed their lives to Him so He could be their leader. Many, across the world, have come forward in response to ask Jesus to take away their pain. And yes, Jesus does take away our pain. He does long to be our Savior. He is the epitome of leadership, which is actually servanthood. But in the end He is so much more than that; He is Lord.

Are you lost? Perhaps being lost isn't such a bad thing. Feeling lost may help us realize we've been walking with Jesus but haven't really seen Him. We've been Christians our entire lives, but we're still searching for something. Maybe being lost wakes us up to the fact that bushes are burning, all around us. Maybe, if you feel lost, a good place to start would be this: Every knee will bow and declare not that Jesus is a rabbi, leader, guru, friend or homeboy, but Lord. Who will you say He is?

CHAPTER TWO

Searching for Something

Have you learned to breathe on your own?

It doesn't matter what kind of lost you are—the kind where you know you're lost or the kind where you haven't realized it yet. We're all trying to put our puzzles together. Whether we're building from the wrong picture or the right one, we're all fascinated with the idea of God.

Solomon says in Ecclesiastes 3, "He has also set *eternity in the human heart;* yet no one can fathom what God has done from beginning to end" (emphasis mine). Solomon acknowledges—in the same breath—that the idea of eternity and God is planted in the human heart and also that God is far too big for our comprehension. Fascination is a predisposition.

Consider what happens any time you bring up the topic of God at work or school. Suddenly the conversation comes alive. If people weren't paying attention before, they're paying attention now. Everyone has thoughts, ideas, questions, and opinions about God.

Here's the thing: Jesus is comfortable with our fascination. He isn't offended at our questions. In fact, of the one hundred and twenty-five incidents in Scripture where Jesus teaches, thirteen of them start with content and the rest with questions. It's okay to question things. Sometimes questions tell us more than answers.

Starting from an early age, I was fascinated with God. My parents divorced when I was young. Obviously, as a kid, it isn't cool for your parents to split up. Like any kid, I felt uncertain and at times unsettled. But after the divorce, I would stay with my dad on the weekends. So the consolation was I got to have two birthdays and two Christmases, and every time I went to Dad's house, we would eat pizza and nachos and play war games.

For me, the obstacle of wondering if God was real was overcome at a young age. I was very aware of a world beyond the physical one. You didn't have to convince me of it or coerce me to believe it was true. I had experienced it firsthand.

When I was young, I learned from those I was around to explore the spiritual realms. From eastern mysticism, my fascination morphed into conversations with demons—which will take you further than you want to go and keep you longer than you want to stay. I didn't have a compass to guide my journey. I just explored, unanchored and with a deep sense of longing for the fulfillment I hoped I would find. As early as third and fourth grade, I was drinking whiskey, making candles float, and moving chairs with my mind. There were few dark corners of the spirit world I hadn't explored. And still, I knew there was more.

In my teenage years, my fascination with God continued. I can remember wearing my pot leaf T-shirt to chemistry class—showing up high and talking to my physics partner, who I knew was a "church kid," about God. I would ask him questions from time to time and wonder if going to church was something I should try.

In the eighth grade, I did give church a brief try. My family began attending our local Catholic church, and I signed up for catechism classes. I took a break from witchcraft and gave church everything I had. I prayed the rosary regularly, read every book the priest gave us, participated

> No matter how long we've known God, we never know everything there is to know about Him.

in class, and asked more than my share of questions. I went to mass every Sunday. The hunger inside me was so pervasive that a gentleman in the church mentioned I had potential to become a priest. He even offered to pay for my seminary training.

Eventually, I gave up on Catholicism and went back to searching. Looking back now, I see how I could have found Jesus through that experience, but I didn't. When I discovered the priest was an alcoholic, I remember thinking the whole religious thing was a joke. Evidently the coffee cup he'd been carrying around with him wasn't filled with coffee. So I used his hypocrisy and my personal struggles as an excuse to become bitter against the church and everyone in it. We do ourselves a disservice when we look to people to give us the picture of God that only Jesus can give.

Here's the thing. All of us are searching. Proverbs 25:2 says, "It is the glory of God to conceal a matter; to search out a matter is the glory of kings." No matter how long we've known God, we never know everything there is to know about Him. We can come to know Him in a moment—and still spend eternity learning about Him. It's God's glory to conceal these matters from us. It's our glory, as children of the King, to search for them.

Yet those of us who have done our share of searching know: Searching doesn't always feel glorious. When you're searching for God and you don't know where to find Him, it's almost like you can't breathe. Maybe this is one of the ways we can tell if we're lost, if we're short of breath and feel like something is missing. Maybe this is one of the ways we can tell Jesus from all the rest: He helps us find our breath.

Into the Water

In the womb, a baby learns to breathe surrounded by fluid. I think about this each time I read how Jesus summoned Peter out of the boat to become a water-walker. During his moment of drowning, Peter was afraid and Jesus asked, "Why are you afraid?" Peter said, essentially: "I'm drowning! I'm not created to breathe in water."

A few years ago, my wife Ali and I traveled with our two daughters and another family to an amusement park in Florida. We rode the rides, ate the food, and performed the typical American routine. Nothing says America like an overpriced hot dog, long lines, and make-believe superheroes wandering around the great outdoors in tights.

One day during our excursion we decided to visit a water park. Filled with lazy rivers, splash pools, water fountains, and yes, hot dogs, it was a paradise of sorts.

We happened upon an area of the water park where you could put on snorkeling equipment and float among baby sharks and stingrays. An avid swimmer I am not but a proud father I am, so when the other dad we were with innocently suggested the two of us go swim with "wild and dangerous beasts" (they were tiny animals but words like *shark* do elicit a certain kind of fear), we quickly kissed our wives good-bye, placed the equipment in tow, and headed down the pathway to begin the adventure.

Our families were up above the saltwater tank waving at us. I couldn't help but notice the twinkle in my daughters' eyes as they watched their heroic father about to risk his life for yet another family memory. But something peculiar happened before we began snorkeling. A voice came over the loud speaker with clear instructions on what to do and what not to do. I only remember the phrase *"and whatever you do, please do not swim toward or lay on top of the rock in the middle of the tank. Be sure not to splash or swim in the water. Avoid drawing attention to yourself."*

Needless to say, I didn't listen very closely to the instructions. I assumed that snorkeling was easy, and the instructions were a waste of my time. So I paid no attention, nor did I read the steps clearly written at a third-grade level on the large white sign in front of me. I simply placed my gear on my head and waited. For the first time, and the only time since, I was about to snorkel. How hard could it be to stick your face in the water and breathe through a rubber hose while staring at sea life?

Well, for the average human being, it isn't difficult. For me, it became a nightmare. Dozens of raving fans were about to have the show of their lives.

The tank was surrounded by what appeared to be rock formations, including a singular rock, a few feet in diameter, which sat in the center of the tank. We were supposed to float, not swim, which I'm sure had something to do with the sharks. We got the green light to get into the water, and I immediately went for it. Memories of watching Jacques Cousteau as a child on the Public Broadcasting System flooded my mind as I envisioned sharks and stingrays swimming beneath my stomach. I was ready for this. I was made for this. Yet within ten seconds of jumping into the water, I realized I wasn't breathing clean oxygen, but salt water.

By the way, we weren't made to breathe salt water. Within a few seconds I became disoriented. Water lodged in your esophagus isn't a good feeling. I panicked, kicked, and attempted to scream. I flailed around like a goldfish on dry ground. My girls' happy expressions turned to panic as they watched the evolution of superhero dad turned panicked survivor. At the time, I was a fairly muscular guy, but it doesn't matter how much you can bench press when you're drinking salt water like a Slurpee at 7-11. All that matters is oxygen. My only hope of survival (so I thought) was to begin swimming, pawing, and doggy paddling toward the rock in the center of the tank. All I craved were dry land and oxygen.

When someone is in survival mode, nothing else matters.

I made it to the rock, ripped the snorkel gear off of my face, and held on for dear life. I caught a glimpse of my bride and daughters who were watching the entire scene from up top of the tank on a little bridge. Simultaneously, the same loud speaker that provided instructions at the beginning began scolding me, "Sir, please stop swimming in the tank and let go of the rock."

Let go of the rock? That was absurd. I couldn't let go. By now, all of the splashing guaranteed the sharks and stingrays would eat me. Forget about the fact that the sharks were probably only twelve inches long, and I'm sure stingrays don't eat human beings. There was no *way* I was letting go of the rock. I dug in, still in survival mode, and caught another glimpse of my family, who by now, were laughing at me.

"Sir, let go of the rock," the voice echoed. By now, an audience had gathered on the bridge to watch the reason for the overuse of the intercom. I wasn't letting go! You couldn't have made me let go! If they wanted me to let go, they were going to have to get in and help. I wasn't going anywhere until I felt safe again. I needed someone to breathe *for* me. Well, be careful what you wish for.

She jumped off the lifeguard stand, covered in red, with her floatation device. She swam toward the beached whale known as myself, as I clung to the rock. She had a smirk on her face. The gentleman on the intercom needed to relax at this point. "Sir, let go of the rock! Let go of the rock! Stop splashing."

The lifeguard arrived at my side, smiling, and began to pry my hands off the rock. I let go, only to latch onto her red pool noodle and hold on for dear life. I needed to breathe—or someone to breathe for me. I held on as she pulled me to shore. Everyone stared. Some laughed. Ok, *everyone* laughed. I will go down in the record books as that guy who was saved by a girl in the snorkel tank. I single-handedly ruined the snorkeling experience for everyone else.

After a few minutes of vacating the tank, I caught my breath and hovered over the railing. I watched dejectedly as other snorkelers experienced what I didn't. The couple we were on vacation with went into the tank and snorkeled, holding hands, gently wading from one end to the other, beholding the beautiful sea creatures in a fashion that honored *The Little Mermaid* and *Finding Nemo*. As the couple climbed up the steps, dripping wet but smiling, I realized this was my moment and asked Ali if she wanted to snorkel with me. She smiled, and I knew we were in for a treat.

We both gathered our gear and, like any good friend who happens to be my wife, she kindly pointed out, as we stood next to the sign with the rules of the snorkel tank, that I didn't follow the rules! Obviously, she was right. So this time I paid close attention as the voice came over the loud speaker with instructions on how to guarantee an enjoyable experience. I listened. I memorized. I was ready. Rather than plunging into the tank and dipping my entire head under the water as I had before, I slid down the edge of the tank next to Ali and entered the tank with my face dry and oxygen freely flowing.

We grabbed hands and waited for the signal to go. As soon as we were granted permission, I tenderly placed my face in the water as we floated in tandem, hand in hand, upon the water. As luck would have it, however, a kink in my hose prevented air from flowing and I panicked yet again. Did I gather my composure like every other normal human being? No. I dipped my entire head into the salt water again and began to breathe in the very mixture

CHAPTER TWO: SEARCHING FOR SOMETHING

responsible for my first disorientation. Salt water invaded my
mouth, lungs, and for all I know was leaking out my toes.

I let go of Ali's hand and, in my kicking and flailing, hit her in
the face. Just like that, her knight in shining armor became a little
boy before her very eyes. I jerked off the mask and hose and made
a beeline for the rock in the middle of the tank. Before arriving
there, the familiar voice heard over the intercom announced for
the entire amusement park to hear: "Sir,
do not go near the rock. Stop splashing.
Sir . . . Sir . . . Sir!"

I didn't care. I was dying. No I wasn't,
I was panicking and making a spectacle
of myself, but in my justification, I was
dying. I grabbed onto the rock again and
held on for dear life. The same lifeguard
who saved me before jumped in, smiling from ear to ear, and
swam toward me for yet another rescue. Without offering any
assistance, I allowed her to tow me again safely to shore. Ali
stayed in the tank with the rest of the normal people and enjoyed
her snorkel.

> Faith is not
> a safety
> from the
> treacherous
> parts of life.

I realized in that moment that I'm not cut out for snorkeling —
at least until I can have some training in the kiddie pool in my
backyard away from other living beings. Additionally, I learned
that it is *not* normal to stick your face in the water and breathe. I
can relate to Peter. I know what it feels like to be drowning. I don't
blame him for being scared.

Holding the Wrong Rock

Jesus is always with us, but this doesn't mean we're always aware of Him. Too often, we miss Him because we're holding onto the wrong rock. If we're going to find Jesus, we must go to places where comfort is a bygone experience. We wave good-bye to it in the rearview mirror. He leads us upon the water. He beckons us. He calls us to stop grasping for the things we think are saving us and instead reach out to hold onto Him.

Too many of us forget, in our search for God, that faith isn't a program for controlling our experiences and circumstances so that we never have to face life's storms. Faith is not a safety from the treacherous parts of life. There *is* a place of safety and a place of rest when we follow Jesus, but that safety and rest come most profoundly when we realize our safety isn't found in circumstances but in His divine presence.

He calls us onto the water. Matthew 14:26–33 says, "But immediately Jesus spoke to them, saying, 'Take heart; it is I. Do not be afraid . . . Come'" (ESV). So Peter got out of the boat and walked on the water and came to Jesus. At other times, He calls us to go *through* the water. In Exodus 14, rather than call the Israelites to step out onto the water, God led them *into* it. "The LORD said to Moses, 'Why do you cry to me? Tell the people of Israel to go forward. Lift up your staff, and stretch out your hand over the sea and divide it, that the people of Israel may go through the sea on dry ground'" (Ex. 14:15, ESV).

Can you imagine? The Hebrews were emancipated and finally free from human trafficking in Egypt. They had suffered unspeakable oppression and injustice. They feared they would never be free. They feared freedom would be death for them. And yet in this profound movement of God, He miraculously rescued them.

What are we supposed to do as we search for God and He calls us out upon the water? How are we supposed to find our security when we're in the middle of a storm and it seems there's nothing steady to hold onto? How should we respond when our safety seems threatened and we feel compelled to grab the closest rock? There's an answer in the lives of Peter and the Israelites. It goes like this: There's a tension between rest and movement. We have to be willing to do both—rest in God's sovereignty and move forward in faith.

Another way of saying this is that there's a time to *pray* and a time to *obey*. To pray when you need to obey is lazy. To obey when you need to pray first is precocious. Only when we find the balance between these two will we discover what it feels like to breathe even when surrounded by water. Only then will we uncover the incredible comfort of abiding in God in the middle of life's tumultuous circumstances. Only then can we experience the miracle of being held in the peaceful arms of Jesus. Only then can we find what we've been looking for all along.

Scripture says the kingdom is forcefully advancing and that forceful people lay hold of it. Scripture also urges us to be still and know He is God. In Exodus 14, we see that rest isn't necessarily ceasing from "doing"; it's more like a spiritual location, a state of being. In a tumultuous climate, Moses found rest. As we saw in the midst of the storm that distracted Peter, Jesus was able to find this spiritual place of rest as well.

The Israelites stepped into the water and walked confidently forward. Were they afraid? Scripture doesn't tell us they were. The Bible does declare, however, that the waters were afraid. The psalmist recounts the incident: "The waters saw you, God, the waters saw you and writhed; the very depths were convulsed" (77:16). The waters literally writhed in fear at the power of God. Amazing!

Sometimes when God calls us onto the water His footprints remain unseen. His path is no less sturdy, though it remains concealed and unannounced.

What would happen if we moved beyond the point of fear of drowning and simply stepped into the water? What if we refused to allow our environment to define who God is to us? What if, instead of cowering in fear of our questions, we fostered the tension between rest and movement? I believe we would see our environment, like the waters of the Red Sea, cower in fear of the greatness of our God.

In the Aramaic Bible translated into plain English, Psalm 89:9 reads: "You are The Ruler in the magnificence of the sea and you stop the tumult of its waves!" When the storms of our lives rage—we lose our jobs, the debt-collectors come, our marriage falls apart, we lose someone we love—God's still in charge of the waves. In Mark's gospel, Jesus said, "Peace be still," and the storm ceased. Elsewhere in the book of Acts, God allowed the storm to rage for fourteen nights before Paul was rescued. There are times when God calms the storm and times when He allows the storm to rage. Why? Because the tumult isn't in the waves but in our response to the waves.

There are moments when the path toward Jesus becomes so difficult we find it hard to breathe. Like Peter, we become afraid. Jesus looks at us and asks: Why are you afraid? After all, He learned to sleep in the bottom of the boat in the midst of a storm. Jesus didn't succumb to the effects of the storm. Instead, the storm was afraid of Jesus.

Even when our paths take us deep into the water, we are safe. We leave our maps at home and pick up His compass and begin to walk. I love what Psalm 77:19 says: "Your way was through the sea, your path through the waters, yet your footprint remained unseen." Sometimes when God calls us onto the water His footprints remain unseen. His path is no less sturdy, though it remains concealed and unannounced. Look beneath you. The ground you walk on in is sacred—even if you haven't noticed it.

From a young age, I had a difficult time "breathing." I look back now and realize I was surrounded by God's presence but unaware of it, like an infant. He was breathing for me. I remember those early days. Tears were common. Questions didn't have words. I learned how to survive. My life felt void of God, even as the bush was burning. I struggled to find a path through the raging waters. But the whole time, He was breathing for me. We weren't created to live in an environment void of Jesus. We were created for life. We were created to step onto the water and, if need be, allow Him to breathe for us.

Learning to Breathe

Many of us are fascinated with God, but fascination isn't enough. Judas was fascinated with God, but he wasn't close to Him. James says even the demons tremble at the thought of God—and that isn't enough. If you're feeling short of breath—if you're terrified because you're living through the middle of a storm and can't see what's coming next—abide in God. Stay close to Him. We need more than a fascination with Him or His power. We need God Himself. *Turn and see* that the bush is always burning.

Abiding in Jesus is different from proximity to Jesus. Judas had proximity to Jesus, but he didn't abide. Judas was there when Jesus called Peter to leave the comfort of the boat and come onto the water. Judas was there when the storm calmed and Jesus re-entered the boat. Judas had all he opportunities the others disciples had. He was as close to Jesus as anyone. But something in his heart just didn't click. Judas had learned how to breathe on his own.

In the church today, some of us do a great job of seeking knowledge, apart from abiding. As a result, our minds are satisfied but our souls are left longing. The bush is burning, but we haven't learned how to notice it. Instead, we've learned how to breathe on our own. Our focus is on what we believe about certain things rather than on *why* we believe—or Who it's all for. Is doctrine important? Absolutely! Does doctrine replace intimacy with Christ? Never!

Any environment without Christ is suffocating. Jesus said in John 10:10, "I have come that they may have life." In this verse, the word Jesus used for *life*, translated in Greek, is *zoe*, meaning "very existence." John also records that after Jesus' resurrection when He appeared to His disciples in the upper room, He breathed new life (the Holy Spirit) on them. "And with that, He breathed on them and said, 'Receive the Holy Spirit'" (John 20:22). The symbolism here is huge. Life in Christ can be described as spiritual breathing, our very life force. Life without Christ is suffocating.

We're all searching. We're all "out on the water," so to speak. The storms are raging. But those without Christ are suffocating. They cannot breathe. If you are *in* Christ, even if you feel as if you're drowning, be assured you're completely safe. He has become your breath. He is breathing for you.

My crazy snorkeling experience offers a graphic picture of what someone looks like when they're created to live in the *"zoe"* environment of Christ but are trying to breathe on their own. It never works. We drown in a stormy sea, having full access to oxygen. Living without air is a horrible feeling. It led Judas to suicide. It's what almost led to mine. I remember now.

CHAPTER THREE

Paving Our Way to Jesus

Do you see the burning bush in front of you?

S everal years ago, acclaimed violinist Joshua Bell famously performed incognito for tips in a Washington DC subway station. This is a man who typically draws finely dressed crowds of thousands to fancy auditoriums. He has won countless awards and accolades for his talent. But that day, he opened his violin case in the middle of a bustling subway station and began to play.

People rushed by on their way to work. They dropped a coin or two or even a bill into his violin case. To them, it was a familiar scene, a routine—no different from the music they usually heard from the variety of roughly dressed people who played instruments there any other day. They didn't realize that one of the world's finest violinists was playing right in front of them. They were so focused on their intended destination that they missed it. Of course, they *heard* the music as they marched along on their daily commute; they simply didn't notice what they heard.

It's easy to write off the familiar, to overlook what's right in front of us. Scripture shares with us that eternity—heaven, hell, God, eternal right and wrong—resides deep within our own hearts, and yet somehow we often miss it. Truth has been carved into our consciousness from the beginning of time and yet we're still searching. Romans 1 reminds us that God and His attributes can be clearly seen. And yet sometimes what's right in front of us is difficult to recognize.

Why does it takes so long for us to realize our need for Jesus—to see how close He has been to us all along? Because we rely on our own resources. We're so focused on our intended destination—like the passersby rushing through their morning commute—that we can't see greatness in our midst. Maybe that's why we tend to meet Jesus when we come to the end of our own proverbial devices.

Joshua Bell—who it turns out was in cahoots with *The Washington Post*—said later that he performed the stunt in the subway station simply to see if anyone would notice. He understands, as much as anyone, how music loses some of its power when it doesn't have an audience. My favorite part of the story is this: Now living in New York City, Bell makes sure to stop and pay attention whenever he hears anyone playing a musical instrument on the street. "I don't want to be the one who walks by and doesn't pay attention," he says.

Neither do I. I don't want to be the kind of person who walks by and doesn't pay attention. The bush always burns, and the ground is always sacred. Jesus is profoundly with us, and yet we often ignore Him. Why?

Normal and Familiar

Each of us learns at a young age what it looks like to get by on our own devices. We figure out how to get what we need and take care of ourselves. We discover how to survive—physically, socially, emotionally, practically. This strategy looks different for each of us depending on our upbringing and background, but these are survival techniques for us. For me, the two biggest techniques were: (1) get good grades and (2) don't mouth off to a parent. As long as I did these things, life was good. I could do just about anything else I wanted.

I threw myself into friends and skateboarding. My life, although confusing in many ways, was also "normal" as far as I knew. It was normal to go to your dad's house on the weekend. It was normal to come home from school and spend the afternoon alone. It was normal to get drunk and high, to study witchcraft and Satanism. Yet what is normal for us often keeps us from recognizing the possibility of something greater. The important often gets lost somewhere in the middle of the familiar.

This is one of the greatest problems with paving our own way to Jesus. We have a limited understanding to draw on.

> What is normal for us often keeps us from recognizing the possibility of something greater. The important often gets lost somewhere in the middle of the familiar.

What we call normal is rarely God's best for us. Our survival tactics, our ways of getting by, our routines and rhythms (spiritual or not) may be effective tools for navigating the physical world, but they're insufficient for traversing a heavenly one. For that journey, only Jesus will do. We're building our puzzle from the wrong picture.

Looking for What God Gives

For years I searched for truth and meaning before I ever discovered it. I would look in every dark corner and under every questionable rock. I never discriminated when it came to the places I was willing to explore. I only wish I had known I didn't need to travel far and wide in search of Truth; He was right in front of me. He's always within reach. Jeremiah 29:13 says, "You will seek me and find me when you seek me with all of your heart."

At times it felt like God was playing hide-and-seek. Have you ever felt that no matter how hard you look for Jesus, you can't find Him? That no matter how hard you work to reach Him, you can't get there? I remember hearing someone say, "God doesn't hide things from us; He hides things *for* us." Proverbs 25:2 fleshes out this idea: "It is the glory of God to conceal a matter; to search out a matter is the glory of kings." When we find ourselves wondering if God is playing hide-and-seek with us, Proverbs reminds us that He calls us "royalty," and that our longing to find Him is an indicator of how much He loves us.

The problem comes because so many of us—myself included, in that time of my life—are not seeking God. We're seeking the results of God. We're seeking peace or love or significance or value or blessing. Matthew is clear: Seek first the kingdom, and the rest will be added. Only when we surrender the things we think we want do we discover what we truly wanted all along. Apart from Jesus, we find only a counterfeit of peace, love, and significance. When poison is dipped in chocolate, it only offers a better brand of misery. Meanwhile, we're missing the acts of heaven unfolding all around us.

Bite-Sized Pieces

If I were God, and I were coming to the earth for the first time in the flesh to introduce myself to humanity, I would make it simple. Everyone would receive an invitation to an event where all of the angels would stand in unison, all doubts would be relieved, all diseases cured, every social dilemma solved, all sin exposed, and my presence would engulf everyone. I would perform a few miracles and leave a coherent belief system. Why not summon the universe and draw a line in the sand to eradicate anything that might counter my plan for creation?

Jesus didn't do this. He was a Hebrew. His native tongue was Aramaic, yet His teachings were recorded in Greek. Greek? Why? If His goal was clarity, speaking Greek wasn't the most advantageous decision. Jesus spent three and a half years transitioning the entire world from the Old Covenant to the New Covenant. Yet, He didn't leave behind a coherent belief system. All He left was Himself.

I've always liked what pastor and author (leader of *The Message* translation) Eugene Peterson said—that Jesus came to teach us not *what* to think, but *how* to think. Rather than explain

Are you busy looking for Jesus while He's sitting right in front of you?

things in a clear, orderly way, He took eternal truth and covered it in story. He told parables to draw each person to Himself. His first sermon was, "Repent, for the kingdom of heaven is at hand." I can imagine His audience saying to themselves, *What does that mean?* It wasn't a three-point sermon. He didn't leave them with an actionable takeaway. He left them wanting more, even feeling a little uneasy.

Consider for a minute the implications of this approach and how it changes the way we engage our faith today. So many of us are focused on taking what Jesus taught and breaking it into bite-sized pieces and manageable steps, when even Jesus Himself wasn't concerned with that. Are you busy looking for Jesus while He's sitting right in front of you?

Can you imagine if the disciples had missed what Jesus wanted them to understand because they were concerned about the "rules" they were supposed to follow? Matthew 17 records the moment when Jesus revealed Himself as God to three of His disciples. He took them up on a mountain, where He was transfigured (Matt. 17:2). His face shone, His clothes glowed, and Moses and Elijah appeared to talk to Him. The disciples were terrified. Can you blame them? Something truly profound had taken place right in front of them. "But Jesus came and touched them, saying, 'Rise, and have no fear.' And when they lifted up their eyes, they saw no one but Jesus only" (Matt. 17:7–8, ESV).

At this point, it had to be abundantly clear to those three disciples that Jesus was no ordinary man. Heaven opened in front of them as Moses and Elijah stood there, talking with Jesus. In one brief moment, Jesus cleared away all distractions and showed Himself clearly. But notice what happened only minutes after this experience.

> As they were coming down the mountain, Jesus commanded them, "Tell no one the vision, until the Son of Man is raised from the dead." And the disciples asked him, "Then why do the scribes say that first Elijah must come?" He answered, "Elijah does come, and he will restore all things. But I tell you that Elijah has already come, and they did not recognize him, but did to him whatever they pleased. So also the Son of Man will certainly suffer at their hands." Then the disciples understood that he was speaking to them of John the Baptist. (Matt. 17:9–13, ESV)

Did you catch that? Jesus just communicated, more clearly than ever before, exactly what would happen in the coming months. It was the crux of the gospel: The Son of God would be betrayed and killed. He would suffer and die. He explained how He was the Messiah. Were the disciples paying attention as Jesus gave them this invaluable information? We don't have any evidence in this passage to suggest otherwise, but we do know how Peter, James, and John choose to respond *later*.

Peter took out his sword and cut off the ear of one of the men who came to arrest Jesus. I wonder if Peter's response would have been different in the garden of Gethsemane if he had listened more intently on the mount of transfiguration. I wonder what aspects of the conversation Peter missed between Jesus, Elijah, and Moses because he was too concerned with what he was going to say. If you read the passage in its entirety, you'll notice Peter, who wasn't asked a question, sought to provide an answer to God. That's when a loud voice thundered and Peter, along with James and John, heard the audible voice of the Father and the instruction to listen to Jesus.

> We simply need to slow down from our routine and rhythm and fix our attention on the profound acts of heaven happening all around us.

How often does this happen to us—a profound encounter with Jesus unfolds right in front of us, but we miss it? We're too concerned with our own agenda, with the distractions around us, with the rules, with our routine—or with what we want to say. A conversation is happening in heaven *right now* that we're unaware of. If we listen closely, we can hear the same voice that echoed when the universe was crafted. Much like Peter, we miss out on that conversation because we're answering questions that no one, including Jesus, ever asked us. The music is playing, the bush is burning, and we walk right on by.

The "rules," the religious routines, the step-by-step process, our own survival tactics or morality—none of these can lead us to the Jesus we've been searching for. Instead, we can look beneath our feet, where the ground is already and *always has been* sacred. We can stop fighting to be right about the "issues"; we can quit working hard to check off all the boxes. We simply need to slow down from our routine and rhythm and fix our attention on the profound acts of heaven happening all around us.

Slow Down

In his subway experiment, violinist Joshua Bell proved that the simple things are easy to overlook. In my case, it was the simplest thing that revolutionized my life. But before I tell you about that, I want to share a story from Acts 3 that does an amazing job of demonstrating exactly what it looks like to slow down enough to find God in the everyday moments.

In Acts 3, Jesus used Peter to perform an amazing miracle. Peter was going to the temple with John for a time of prayer when he bumped into a man who had been lame since birth. Every day, someone carried the man to the temple gates, where he begged from those going into the temple courts. Scripture says, "When he saw Peter and John about to enter, he asked them for money. Peter looked straight at him, as did John . . ." (Acts 3:3–4).

Then Peter said, "Silver or gold I do not have, but what I do have I give you. In the name of Jesus Christ of Nazareth, walk" (Acts 3:6). Taking the lame man by the hand, Peter helped him up, and instantly the man's feet and ankles became strong. He jumped to his feet and began to walk. When the crowd saw this, of course they had tons of questions. But Peter responded by asking a few questions of his own:

"Fellow Israelites, why does this surprise you? Why do you stare at us as if by our own power or godliness we had made this man walk? The God of Abraham,

Isaac and Jacob, the God of our fathers, has glorified his servant Jesus. . . . By faith in the name of Jesus, this man whom you see and know was made strong. It is Jesus' name and the faith that comes through him that has completely healed him, as you can all see." (Acts 3:12, 16)

A few things are important to notice about this story. The first thing is Peter's willingness to *slow down*. He wasn't too busy, too preoccupied, or too focused on his own destination (although it was a good one—he was going to pray) to stop and have an encounter with God. It's a little ironic, when you think about it, that Peter was *on his* way to have an encounter with God in prayer, and yet God chose to encounter *him* on the way. Sometimes encountering God looks different than we expect it to. Anytime we slow down enough to touch one another, to meet a need—we discover and unveil His majesty.

In some ways this was just another ordinary day for Peter. He had been there during the feast of Pentecost in Acts 2 when the miraculous was displayed. He was there in Acts 2:42–47 when a community on earth formed the first church representing the DNA of heaven. Peter saw the miracles Jesus performed. He had been an eyewitness to Jesus' entire miraculous ministry. Did Peter see and experience things we haven't? Maybe. Maybe not. He understood—in a profound way—that the bush was always burning.

What would have happened if Peter had become desensitized to the miraculous in his life because it was no longer unusual? I wonder how often we miss the miraculous in our lives because we perceive it as ordinary. Sometimes the difference between ordinary and *extra*ordinary is taking the time to see how beautiful ordinary can be.

The second thing I want you to notice about this account is that the miracle is *not* the purpose of the story. The miracle never is. The point of the story is the way the miracle revealed Jesus; and Peter made sure the crowd knew this when they responded with shock and awe. Essentially, he said to them, "Why are you so shocked? You shouldn't be. This is God. This is what God does."

> When we're willing to slow down and tune into those around us—not dismissing the miraculous but rather expecting it—we, too, will come face-to-face with God Himself.

Consider the story of David and Goliath. This isn't a story of a small, weak man who happened to beat up a giant. It's a story of God who is with us in our battles, who takes what is common (a slingshot) and uses it to defeat our giants. God—not David—is the hero in that story. And God is present in our stories as much as He was in David's.

In the book of Daniel, God miraculously rescued a man thrown in a pit with lions. The center of the story is not Daniel; it is God. Through Daniel's story, we discover the bigger story of how God can miraculously deliver us from a hopeless situation, and at the same time, let us live in the midst of another difficult one. Daniel was delivered from the lions' mouths but still lived in a culture hostile to the Hebrew faith. He was still subject to the king responsible for murdering his relatives. God is present even in our most dire circumstances.

All signs and events can point us toward Jesus' presence. When we're willing to slow down and tune into those around us—not dismissing the miraculous but rather expecting it—we, too, will come face-to-face with God Himself.

Our Cup Runs Over

Like Peter in Acts 3, if you slow down long enough to notice, you'll discover a table prepared for you. A banqueting table is spread and God has invited all of us—you, me, and those we would never expect. If anyone knows how to throw a party, it's God. Not only does He invite us to a feast even in the midst of the storms and battles of our lives, but Psalm 23 says He also anoints our heads with oil and our cups run over.

Do you understand how beautiful this is? Let me paint you a picture.

Think about the nomadic tribes of biblical times and what life in the desert was like for them—no way to bathe regularly . . . insect bites . . . poisonous predators. We have evidence of both the medicinal and aromatic value of essential oils used at that time in history. The oils provided basic hygiene, offered relief to those unable to bathe for days in the desert, and could kill head lice. It was customary for travelers to approach a camp for much needed food and water. In Middle-Eastern tradition, the host was responsible to provide protection, nourishment, and most importantly, hospitality for his guests.

If I were a traveler in those days, I would approach your tent. As a good host, you would provide oil for my head, materials to cleanse my feet, and you would invite my family and me to recline and share a meal with you. The conversation would likely involve hearing each other's stories and practicing the ancient art of musing (see Ps. 77:11). The shepherds would take their staffs, covered with carvings of the miracles they'd seen over the past years, and roll them around, recounting testimony after testimony of the miraculous things that had taken place.

At the end of the meal, the unwritten custom of the day was for the head of the house to get up and approach the traveler with drink in hand. The traveler would hold his cup and wait. If the host filled the cup halfway, that was his polite way of saying, "The company is fabulous, but you and your family must leave now." If the cup was filled all the way to the top, the host silently and emphatically declared, "We so enjoy your company, we invite you to spend the evening with us, and in the morning before you depart, we will share one more meal."

Do you see what happens in Psalm 23? Our host, the Good Shepherd, invites us to a banquet. He throws a party—not only in the lush green pasture, where we are surrounded by friends and family, but also in the valley, where we are surrounded by our enemies. We have a choice to focus on our enemies or focus on the banqueting table. Our host anoints our head with oil. Our cup overflows. What some would call waste—the ground drinks up the excess—He calls blessing, a blessing that comes even amidst circumstances where we wouldn't expect to find it.

Stewarding Moments

If you want to know God in the most profound way of knowing—stop seeking the results of God and begin looking for God Himself. He doesn't show up in the rules, the step-by-steps, and the how to's but breaks into our world in the most mundane ways. He's here in the little things, the moments. You won't find Him in duty or morality. In fact, so often it's possible to miss Him in those places, just as Peter would have missed the profound display of God's grace if he hadn't been willing to stop in his rush to get to the temple and ask God to heal a crippled man.

Your day, my day, every day is made up of moments . . . tiny little moments that seem unimportant and predictable. Your alarm goes off. You go to work. You see the same people, every day. You pass people on the street. You sit next to someone in a cubicle. You go to church and brush shoulders with others. Everywhere around you, Jesus is calling out, "I'm here—in the faces and places and stories of these people."

There is healing to be done. There are miracles at work. More than that, Jesus is present in the very inconveniences and roadblocks we complain about. In the interruptions of each day, Jesus found the miracles. He walked slowly through the crowd so those who sought Him could touch Him.

It took me a long time to figure this out. I spent so many years searching and trying to be good enough to chart my way to God. I hope you don't waste as many years as I did. I want you to be awake to the realities of Jesus today. I want your life to be transformed. I want you to become a steward of moments. I want to help you build your picture off of the right puzzle lid.

My story today is far from the one I planned to write. I was lost. I was searching. Somehow, even after years of resisting and looking in the wrong places, I was willing to slow down enough to notice. I was able to see God in the most ordinary moment. Not only that, but as I continue to share my story you'll see that I'm the product of one person who was willing to slow down long enough to see Christ at work in me. The simplest things can revolutionize our lives.

Moments sneak up on us only to unearth a conversation already occurring in heaven. We may have been unaware of the conversation before, but we can choose to be aware now. This conversation carries immense weight in this life. It's a story—and our stories are being written through the same divine hand that flung the stars into space and carved the canyons into the earth. This is your story and my story. His story. History.

At this moment in history, we have a choice. We can become aware of how unaware we've been, or we can continue moving through our duty and routine, choosing not to acknowledge the beautiful music filling the subway station. We can either recognize the sacred ground below our feet, or choose not to *turn and see* the bushes ablaze all around us.

God still performs miracles. I've witnessed many firsthand. I've seen a crippled man in Argentina get up and walk. I've seen a withered hand straighten and be restored. I've seen blind eyes opened and tumors the size of grapefruits disappear. These are stories for believing believers—for those of us who choose to forego the rules, to give up morality and understand our need for Jesus. All it takes is a moment. All it takes is slowing down long enough to listen.

CHAPTER FOUR

Rainmakers

Have you slowed down long enough to hear God's voice?

S ome 282 feet below sea level, Death Valley is known as a place where nothing grows or survives. As the lowest point in the Western hemisphere, the nearby mountains prevent much-needed rainfall from getting there, meaning the soil is rarely ever moist enough to support life. That is, until the winter of 2004, when a record-breaking six inches of rain (in comparison to an average two inches) fell. Then something amazing happened. In the spring of 2005, a quilt of wildflowers bloomed on the valley floor.

Sometimes we assume something isn't possible; we tell ourselves a person, place, or thing isn't "made" for some particular function. We declare a place like Death Valley dead, only to discover it wasn't dead after all—just dormant. It was simply missing one key element: rain. With that element in place, everything changed. The wildflowers bloomed.

Sir Ken Robinson, author and speaker for TED articulated the "dead versus dormant" idea in his 2013 TED talk, "How to Escape Education's Death Valley." Although Robinson used the analogy to talk about the state of education in the United States, I think his words have profound meaning for our spiritual lives. "Right beneath the surface," Robinson assures us, "are seeds of possibility, waiting for the right conditions to come out."[1] It's amazing what a little rain can do, don't you think?

Consider your own spiritual life. Are there people or circumstances that have been the "rain" to your death valley? Maybe you were going through a difficult season and someone simply listened to you. Perhaps someone invited you to an event where you experienced deeper communion with the Savior. Maybe somebody prayed for you behind closed doors, and you didn't even realize it was happening. Who came to you at just the right time and brought much-needed refreshing to your spirit when you were feeling dry? For me, it was a thirteen-year-old girl.

God Speaks

It seems impossible that the prayers of a thirteen-year-old girl could change the course of a destiny and re-route a legacy, but in my case it's true. With the clanging of closing lockers in the hallway of a middle school, a young girl in the eighth grade had a thought in her heart: *Pray for him. You are going to marry him one day. I have a call on his life to preach.* Her courage to respond in that moment would change both of our lives forever.

She was a regular churchgoer. She grew up listening to sermons, singing songs, and amassing information about Jesus. Although she knew of Him, she admittedly didn't really *know* Him. She wasn't paying attention. She was asleep, the way so many Christians are today, the way I've been on many occasions. The realities of heaven were happening all around her, but she wasn't paying attention. And yet the reason such a profound thing could happen in such an ordinary place is because one ill-equipped person was willing to listen.

The Greek New Testament includes two primary words for "know." One means "knowledge based on fact"; the other is "knowledge based on experience."

> When we know Jesus, we listen to Him when He speaks to us, and we are sensitive enough to what He is doing to take part in it.

In our culture, we assume that if someone attends church, they know Jesus. But this isn't necessarily true. Knowing *about* Jesus and truly knowing Him are two separate realities. When we know Jesus, we listen to Him when He speaks to us, and we are sensitive enough to what He is doing to take part in it. Only when we live in communion and experience with Him do we know Him in the most profound way. When God speaks and we listen, incredible things happen.

God speaks to us in many ways. Sometimes He speaks in an audible voice. Other times, He awakens our consciences. Often He speaks to us through nature, His Word, trustworthy people in our lives, or through circumstances. Hearing God's voice (like seeing a burning bush) is much less about physical hearing than it is about spiritual listening. The more we lean in to listen with our hearts, the more we hear from Him.

The young girl at the lockers that day didn't hear from God because of her spiritual pedigree or upbringing. Candidly, she was unaware that it was the Holy Spirit speaking to her. She heard from Him because God speaks to us all. In that moment, she just happened to slow down long enough to hear His voice. She listened in one of the unannounced moments. When one person turns to see what God has always been doing, it's amazing what can happen. It can be like Peter on his way to pray at the temple; or like the rain that brought life to Death Valley.

This girl and I knew each other casually in junior high. In fact, I would often ask her questions about God, but she would rarely answer. After eighth grade, our journeys took us to different high schools. Over the next three years, I faced death numerous times in my lifestyle of drugs, darkness, and addiction. Her journey, on the other hand, included school, cheerleading, friends, regular church attendance, and a continued place of knowing Jesus without really *knowing* Jesus. Church can be one of the darkest places in the world if we don't really know God.

During her junior year, a youth pastor at her church offered an optional Sunday school class for those interested in growing in their faith. The class required homework, Bible reading, memory verses, and minimal absences. It was for students who were *serious* about truly knowing Jesus.

This young girl—now not quite so young—signed up for the class, telling herself, *I've never really given Jesus a chance.*

She started reading the gospel of John and journaling her experience. Within the first few days, she fell in love. John 3:16–17 clearly showed her the depth of God's love. In John 4, we read that Jesus walked approximately twenty-six miles out of His way to have a conversation with a woman (something rabbis didn't do) who was divorced (something Hebrew males didn't do) and who was drawing water from a well in a public place (which no secure religious person could have done). How could the young girl *not* fall in love with this Jesus? She couldn't help but be drawn to such deep love.

As a junior in high school, this young girl met Jesus in the pages of the New Testament, and for the first time in her life wanted to abandon everything to follow Him. Being around Christians her entire life wasn't enough for her. Going to church wasn't enough. What she needed was to *know* Jesus. Once she began to know Him, it changed everything.

Suddenly, she was more aware of His presence. She started seeing Him all around her and hearing the sound of His voice. She couldn't stop reading His Word. She found herself wanting

> Hearing His voice, regardless of how intangible it can be, often comes at inconvenient times and amidst unsuspecting circumstances.

to simply *be* with Him without an agenda or a list of requests. All her dreams, all her priorities seemed to pale in comparison to what God called her to do. The gospel has a way of doing this. Abiding in Him leads to abandonment. We abandon all we have, let go of everything our clenched fists hold dearly, and give up trying to control our lives. When Jesus comes, nothing else matters.

Hearing His voice, regardless of how intangible it can be, often comes at inconvenient times and amidst unsuspecting circumstances. We don't have to listen. He never forces us. But obedience is really as simple as this: hearing a voice and responding in kind. This is truly as spiritual as life in Christ gets. We are called by a voice. His sheep know His voice.

The gospel we read in John 14:23 ("If you love me, keep my commands") is the same gospel we're called to live out. It's similar to what Moses experienced when he responded to the subtle voice of God—a burning bush—leading him to an unsuspecting circumstance. That's what one young girl did that day: nothing too difficult, nothing too profound. And at the same time it was the most beautiful and profound thing she could have done. But I'll tell you more about that later.

Just Fifty-Seven Cents

It doesn't take much to change the course of history, to move the heart of God or to re-route a legacy. It doesn't take much to bring life to the depths of Death Valley: just a little bit of rain, a little bit of money, a little bit of faith. A very little can go a very long way. The bush is always burning, and the ground is always sacred.

At the turn of the twentieth century, a little girl stood near a small church weeping. She had been turned away because it was too crowded. The pastor happened to walk past her as she cried. Clearly, she came from poverty. Her clothes were torn and tattered. She wasn't the type of person to attend a prestigious church such as this one. The pastor took her by the hand and walked her to Sunday school and placed her in a seat. The young girl had the time of her life, and that night went to bed thinking about all the little children who had no place to worship Jesus.

Two years later, the girl's body was found lifeless; a hard life and illness had taken her away. Her parents asked the pastor who had befriended the girl to handle the funeral arrangements. When they moved her body, they found a stained, tattered red purse beside her. Inside were fifty-seven cents and a note saying, "This is to help build the little church bigger so more children can go to Sunday school." For two years, this young girl had been saving this offering of love. The pastor was touched by the faith and compassion of this child who thought her gift was too small. He read her note to the congregation and challenged the deacons to get busy raising money for a larger building.

Meanwhile, a newspaper got hold of the story and published it. Soon after reading the moving article, a wealthy realtor offered the church a choice piece of property worth many thousands of dollars, and when the church asked about the price, the realtor quickly responded "fifty-seven cents." Soon, people from all over began to give to the project, and the young girl's fifty-seven cents turned into over $250,000—a massive sum one hundred years ago.

If you're ever in Philadelphia, look up Temple Baptist Church, which seats 3,300, and Temple University, where hundreds of students are trained. Have a good look, too, at the Good Samaritan Hospital and the Sunday school building large enough that all of the children in the neighborhood can come. And as you walk down the hallway of that Sunday school building, slow down just enough to notice the picture of the sweet face of that little girl—if it's still hanging there—who took her meager fifty-seven cents, placed it in God's hands, and watched it multiply.

It's the fruit of a young child who slowed down long enough to notice some spare change and to share God's vision for it. It's so simple. It's so small. But something most overlooked, she saw. Something unannounced, she heard.

She slowed down long enough to think of other children who needed Sunday school. Peter slowed down long enough to notice the beggar, and God used him to perform a miracle. The thirteen-year-old girl from my junior high school slowed down long enough to pray for a friend, and as you'll see, this laid the groundwork for her life to come. None of them—the young girl, Peter, the student—had much to give. They were all simply willing to notice what God had been busy doing around them all along. What we think is common is actually the miraculous in shroud.

Are You a Rainmaker?

We walk through the office or school or neighborhood, and underneath our feet is dormancy. We share conversations on the way through our daily activities, only to ignore that each space we stand on spiritually is saturated with the seeds of new life. One of my favorite descriptions of Jesus of Nazareth comes from Isaiah 53:2, "a root out of dry ground." Jesus brings life out of nothing and points to the spiritual dormancy of everyone created in His image.

If we will become the rain in the dry place, God will send the blooms.

That eighth-grade girl stood in the hallway of my school, and underneath her feet was anything but dead ground. Little did she know that God was about to send the rain into her life as well. His shadow extended far beyond what she saw when she heard Him say to her, *Pray for him. You are going to marry him one day. I have a call on his life to preach.*

CHAPTER FIVE

It Matters What You Call Yourself

Do you know who you are in Jesus?

Picture this: Jesus is on a boat with His disciples, and suddenly a storm breaks out. The disciples begin to panic. They're afraid for their lives. They frantically look for Jesus and find Him sleeping in the bottom of the boat. They wake Him, terrified, and within minutes He calms the storm. The entire group has just come from the region of Galilee, where they've watched Jesus touch thousands and perform countless miracles. Yet in an instant—when the waves get choppy—they forget whom they're with.

These are the guys who have walked more closely with Jesus than anyone else—but in this moment they demonstrate how lost they still are. They know Jesus, but they're still learning to *know*

Him. When we truly know Jesus, we come to know ourselves as well. And when we come to know ourselves, we no longer lose our cool in the midst of storms.

At this point in the New Testament (Mark 5), news of Jesus' work spread quickly. Crowds of thousands gathered regularly, marveling at Him. Scripture reveals two reasons the people marveled at Jesus: the way in which He spoke and the miracles He performed. Isn't it amazing how quickly people both then and now fall in love with Jesus for what He *does* rather than who He is? When we put all the emphasis on performance, we miss the essence of people, of Jesus. We miss the essence of ourselves.

What Is Your Name?

Jesus left the multitude in Galilee only to encounter another multitude—not a multitude scattered across the landscape, like the previous one, but a multitude embedded within one broken individual: a multitude of demons, a multitude of regrets, and a multitude of missed opportunities. Jesus arrived on the shores of a region known as the Decapolis, or ten cities. As Scripture records, this was His first trip there.

The man Jesus encountered had been demon-possessed for years. No one develops a condition as decrepit as this man overnight. Years of baggage had paved his path. Chances are he had worn the same clothes all that time. He was likely covered in scaly, oozing sores. The Bible tells us he cried out day and night (the Greek word for cry, *krazo*, means "to scream or shriek"). He also cut himself (*katakopto*), literally, "hacked" himself. His behavior was not only incredibly destructive to himself but was a problem for the nearby townsfolk.

The people of the region had tried to help him, sort of. Only their version of help was to bind him with chains and attempt to tame him. Their goal was not so much to help the man as it was to fix the problem he had become for them. Unfortunately, their tactics didn't work. His condition grew stronger than the chains that bound him, and a human being with a story and a name became relegated to a circus sideshow. This man needed people to roll up their sleeves and help him. Instead, their approach was to modify his behavior.

> No amount of pain or torment can keep a person from acknowledging their need for Jesus. His love is undeniable.

Someone once said we don't memorize Jesus; we become like Him. Seeking to demonstrate likeable behavior rather than seeking love is dangerous—especially as we work out our identities. When we teach people to act like Christians without becoming like Christ, we destroy their identity.

It might not seem like it, but we have a lot to learn about identity from this demon-possessed man, who wore nothing but scabs and dried blood. He found his home in the limestone caves of Gadara, rumored to be a frequent place of criminals and the demonized, and considered haunted by the inhabitants. You and I would be repulsed to step foot in this place, let alone live there. This man was the least clean, the least put-together, and the least liked person in the area. Yet when Jesus arrived on shore, the man ran to Him.

Think how crazy this was. In this man's day, many young Jewish men had memorized hundreds of Scripture passages by the time they were adolescents—without actually knowing God. This man was the antithesis of everything a Jewish man should be; yet when God arrived on the shores, he was the one who came running. The townspeople didn't run to greet Jesus; the only hospitality came from a man bound by darkness.

It makes me wonder what this man knew or heard about Jesus that caused him to run toward the Master. It also makes me think how no amount of pain or torment can keep a person from acknowledging their need for Jesus. His love is undeniable. The moment the man known as Legion saw Jesus from far away, he worshipped Him—and the demons that possessed him paid the Lord homage.

As incredible as this seems, Jesus' response is even more amazing. What would you do if a man covered in pus, blood, and scabs, with no clothes on ran screaming directly toward you? I can tell you what I would do: immediately look for the Taser. Jesus simply looked at the man and asked a simple question (Mark 5:9): "What is your name?"

That's incredible! First, I have to imagine that Jesus already knew the man's given name. After all, He's Jesus. The second reason I find this question so fascinating is because it gives an incredible amount of dignity to a man who otherwise had very little. The question "What is your name?" humanizes a person. It moves them out of "demon-possessed" into a position of humanity. With every name comes a story. In Scripture, names carried prophetic significance and historical backdrops. Jesus acknowledged that this man had a story worth hearing.

For all the years he had been possessed, the community tried to tame him, to bind him, and to tolerate him. They needed him to conform. Jesus didn't do any of that. He simply asked the man's name, to which the man replied, "Legion," because so many demons had gone into him (Luke 8:30).

Note the cultural language of this chapter. Scholars believe that because of the language this man used, he must have been a Jew. Yet he was everything a Jew shouldn't have been—naked, exposed, hurting, overlooked, and possessed with 6,000 demons (the number of men in a Roman legion). Some scholars believe that in verse 10, it is the man rather than the demons, who begs Jesus not to send the demons out of the region. This man was hurting so much that the company of thousands of demons was better than being shrouded with the stares of people who knew Scripture in their heads but didn't know God in their hearts. This man was totally confused about who he was.

Chances are you've never been possessed by 6,000 demons. You've probably never even been possessed by one demon. But I'm guessing you may know what it feels like to be pulled in a thousand different directions. Or you know what it feels like to be so lonely you'd prefer to spend time with someone who isn't good for you rather than go home one more night by yourself. You may even know what it feels like to be confused about who you are and why you matter.

People have tried to change you without getting to know you. You know the pain of feeling like you don't belong. You've felt like a nuisance, a bother. You've felt like you're in the way.

You've felt as if no one recognizes you anymore. You can identify with this tormented man—having shared the experience of the inner craving for love.

No matter who you are and what kind of darkness you've suffered, it matters what you call yourself. People will try to tame you, they will try to modify your behavior, but when you encounter love Himself, He will ask you: "What is your name?" And hopefully you will run to Him, no matter how tattered the clothes you are wearing, no matter your spiritual condition. It only takes one touch to be changed by Jesus. We're transformed in an instant, and miraculously, that transformation continues forever.

Who Am I?

As a second grader, my life consisted of the bare essentials: Cheetos, grape Crush soda pop, and the *G.I. Joe* cartoon show after school. We lived a block from my elementary school and after school ended at 3:05, I quickly vacated the property in time to arrive home at 3:10 and watch the remaining twenty minutes of *G.I. Joe*. One night before going to bed, I saw a commercial filled with fighter jets, tanks, and a battle fit for a king. The next *G.I. Joe* episode to air was a can't-miss, and I was determined to make it home as quickly as possible the next day.

The next day came, and my determination had multiplied. The bell rang, I raced out of class and down the hall, and ran outside, darting into the street. Strategically, I hadn't brought a coat with me that day, or a backpack. I knew those things would only slow me down. I also knew I was supposed to go to the corner and wait for the crossing guard who would blow the whistle, stop traffic, and usher me safely across the street. But in my *G.I. Joe* frenzy, I made the decision to ignore this rule and simply cross on my own . . . anything to save time.

I didn't even look out of the corner of my eye to see if any cars were coming. I had an appointment with *G.I. Joe* that could not be rescheduled. So I did what any reasonable human being would do: I closed my eyes and ran across the busy street oblivious to whether or not cars were there. The Mazda RX-7, black in color, slammed on its brakes about the same time it collided with my leg and hip, and a choir of squealing tires sang its prelude to what became a symphony of torture. I flew through the air and landed on the concrete.

It only took a few seconds before I realized two stark contrasts. First, I was not in front of my television, eating Cheetos, waiting for my cartoon; and second, three elderly women—one of whom was hairier than my father—were upon me, draping wool blankets over me like fertilizer.

"You're in shock, baby," one of them said. "Don't move. The ambulance is on its way."

"In shock" was an understatement. *Of course I was in shock. How dare a vehicle get in the way of my plans! How dare these ladies hold me on the ground, against my will, as my entire elementary school gathered to watch the ordeal. And the blankets? Where did these blankets come from? Who carries blankets in their purses? And why am I covered in them on a September afternoon when it's arguably ninety degrees out in the great state of Iowa?*

My questions soon turned to screams as I tried to talk the ladies into letting me go, to no avail. The sirens quickly followed, and I found myself being placed on a stretcher, moved about ten feet, and then quickly examined for any injuries. They poked me, prodded me, and tickled me (unintentionally, I'm sure). Hundreds of students, teachers and parents formed a half moon on the side of the curb. Little did they know they were about to see a *full moon* in the afternoon over the skies of Iowa.

In the ambulance, the EMT worker asked me to stand up, dropped my pants ,and inspected my pelvis. Now, I'm ticklish— very ticklish—so as the inspection began, I jerked around and the EMT worker bumped the big, swinging double doors of the ambulance. They flung wide open. There I stood with my hands around my ankles, pants on the floor and bare bottom exposed to the masses. Although my pelvis wasn't broken, my reputation sure was. Needless to say, the crowd saw a side of me I wasn't proud of. This was a part of my identity I would've preferred to remain anonymous. For the rest of the year, I was known as the kid who showed his bare bottom to the masses. Even *G.I. Joe* wasn't worth that.

This isn't the story of a TV-watching, injured and embarrassed second grader so much as it is the story of all our lives. All of us are searching to know who we are and why we matter, and yet too many of us are looking in the wrong places. We're looking to brand names, awards, family, upbringing, or education. We're looking to skills or training or good deeds or the number of followers we have on Instagram. We look at the ways we fall short or the mistakes we've made and worry that our identity is in question. But Jesus longs for us to run to Him, like Legion did. When we arrive on the shore, Jesus simply looks at us and asks, "What is your name?"

Misplaced Identity

Too many of us search far and wide for our identity when it has been right in front of us all along. The bush is always burning, and the ground is always sacred.

By the time I got to high school, all whisperings of my bare-bummed moment had faded into the past. I got good grades. I partied with the cool kids and, for the most part, was liked by my teachers. But in the deepest part of me, I still felt like something was missing. I didn't feel like I belonged. I asked questions about God constantly, to whoever would listen. I was wondering and searching. And the need for belonging was so powerful that I was willing to do just about anything to fit in.

I was a sophomore when an infamous gang migrated to town. I started hanging out with these guys and found the free beer and access to drugs appealing. To belong required an initiation. It was definitely a price to pay, but the reward was community, belonging. Gangs are all about identity. They make the people who join feel like they belong, like they're protected and part of a family. It always intrigued me how gang members stood by each other. To this day, I still look for this type of community in churches. Sometimes I find it.

At one point, I was close to being initiated into the gang. But the brutality of the final initiation made me uncomfortable enough that I decided not to go forward with it.

We'll never know who we are or why we matter until we meet Jesus.

Still, one night I was hanging with these guys, getting really drunk, like usual. We were over at one of their houses, and a few of us started to get sick. For a while, I lay on the couch, hoping the feeling would pass, but eventually I decided it would be better if I tried to make it home. I was too intoxicated to drive, so I asked a friend to take me home.

The next day my friends and I heard that an opposing gang had driven by that house about fifteen minutes after I had left and opened fire. The couch where I had been lying was obliterated with bullet holes. I should have been dead.

We go to profound lengths to discover our identity. Meanwhile, it's right in front of us. We want to belong somewhere. We want to fit in. We want to matter. The truth is we'll never know who we are or why we matter until we meet Jesus. Colossians 3:3 says, "For you died, and your life is now hidden with Christ in God." Our identity is in Christ. When we meet Jesus, we discover who we are.

Who are you? This simple question may be one of the most important you ever ask yourself, and how you answer it may indicate where you are going. Most of us don't spend nearly enough time trying to discover the answer.

Some of us search for a misplaced identity in drugs or alcohol, but many of us search for ourselves in less dramatic, but equally destructive, ways. We look to those around us to affirm our existence. We lean on our imperfect parents or our broken spouses. We look to Twitter or Facebook to confirm that we matter. Yet no matter how seemingly harmless the source, the damaging effects of looking for your identity somewhere other than in God never changes. Like Legion, when Jesus asks who

CHAPTER FIVE: IT MATTERS WHAT YOU CALL YOURSELF

you are and what your name is, your answer is different than what it should be.

Until you know Jesus—not just "know" Him but really *know* Him—you'll never know who you are, either. You'll always be building your puzzle from the wrong picture. Whether you know it or not, you'll always be a little bit lost.

Looking for Validation

One of the greatest dangers of not knowing who we are is that we try to validate our identity by any means necessary. We act in ways that don't make sense. We self-destruct. That's what happened to Judas; it happens to celebrity after celebrity in our culture. It's what happened to me with the gang, and it's what can happen to all of us—even the most spiritually mature among us—if we aren't careful. The first question Jesus asked Legion was, "What's your name?" It's so important to know who we are.

If I had to put my finger on one thing preventing many modern-day Christians (myself included, at times) from an encounter with the living God, it would be that we're looking for our identity in the wrong places. We're searching for someone or something to validate us. Renowned author C. S. Lewis once said, "All that we call human history—money, poverty, ambition, war, prostitution, classes, empires, slavery—[is] the long terrible story of man trying to find something other than God, which will make him happy."[1] With our hearts wide open, may we honestly assess if we're trying to construct our own identity or if we're looking to Him.

Self-promotion almost always points to a lack of identity.

It's tempting to believe we can "be whoever we want to be." It's even more alluring to think the control is in our hands. No wonder so many of us get sucked in. But as long as we're trying to construct our image from something other than Jesus—the picture of culture around us, magazines, social media, celebrity culture, reality TV—we'll always be missing who God made us to be. We'll be building our puzzle from the wrong picture. It may sound cliché, but remember the saying, "God created you to be an original. Please don't become a counterfeit."

Judas is a prime example. Remember, Judas was close with Jesus. He walked with Jesus on a daily basis. Jesus trusted Judas. Judas was in the "inner circle." From the outside looking in, you would think Judas had a strong sense of purpose and belonging. You would think he *knew* Jesus and therefore knew himself. Of course when we look more closely we see Judas fighting to be seen, to be heard, and to be important—a clear indication that he didn't know himself after all and he hadn't experienced a profound encounter with Christ.

Self-promotion almost always points to a lack of identity. James 3:16 says, "For where you have envy and selfish ambition, there you find disorder and every evil practice." This is profound and provocative: "every evil practice." The same motivation and moral depravity behind child trafficking, pornography, murder, ethnocide, greed, and slander are present wherever selfish ambition is in control. If you want to magnetically attract hell, just be motivated by selfishness.

In the book of John, Mary anointed Jesus with oil and Judas protested. He actually chastised Mary, complaining that her act was poor stewardship, unwise, and overly zealous. John 12:4–6 says:

> But one of his disciples, Judas Iscariot, who was later to betray him, objected, "Why wasn't this perfume sold and the money given to the poor? It was worth a year's wages." He did not say this because he cared about the poor, but because he was a thief; as keeper of the money bag, he used to help himself to what was put into it. (ESV)

At first glance, it could seem that Judas' criticism might be valid. It could be viewed as the responsible and reasonable—even godly—approach. But God saw Judas' heart, and Scripture makes it clear that Judas wasn't trying to be charitable or even reasonable. Rather, he had a habit of robbing the finances of Jesus' ministry for his personal gain.

Who would do such a thing? The answer to that question is simple, but unnerving: you . . . me . . . all of us. When we don't know Jesus—really *know* Him—and therefore know ourselves, we're only steps away from making a decision equally destructive and sinful. Self-importance is alluringly powerful. I've heard before that if pride can turn an angel into a demon and an archangel into Satan, imagine what it can do to us.

The scariest part of all, for me, is how subtle the divide is between Judas and Jesus. The split was so elusive, so subtle, that not one disciple could have noticed it. None of them pegged

Judas as the betrayer at the Last Supper. This scares me when I look at believers today—or, more importantly, when I look into my own life. Sometimes it's a seemingly unnoticeable fracture in our spiritual bedrock that, if left unchecked, can cause us to do the unthinkable.

There was no lack of commitment on Judas' part. In the Garden of Gethsemane, Jesus asked the disciples to pray, and all of them fell asleep—except Judas. He was incredibly committed. He didn't betray Jesus with his eyes closed. He didn't stumble or meander into it. He knew exactly what he was doing. Judas sought out and seized a personal opportunity at the expense of the murder of Jesus. Selfish ambition put skin on when Judas arrived in the garden.

> Jesus knew His plan and His purpose and stuck with them. He understood, at the end of the day, that He answered to the Father.

Theologian, pastor, and author John Piper says of this moment that Satan possessed Judas, but he didn't take an innocent man captive: "Satan doesn't take innocent people captive. There are no innocent people."[2] Isn't this difficult to admit? There are no innocent people. The choices you make are your choices, and you'll be held responsible for them. If you don't know who you are in Jesus—if you aren't awake to the reality of Him in your life, and if you lack an encounter with the living God—you, me, we're just like Judas.

Think about those you know who walk with Jesus. Think about your own relationship to Him. We're an incredibly responsible group. We have more resources and education and opportunities at our fingertips than ever before. We're hard workers and rugged individualists. From the outside looking in, it might seem like we have it all together. But do we know Jesus— *really* know Him? Are we close with Him? Have we looked to Him for our identity? Or are we building our puzzles with the wrong lids?

Judas used the anointing and purpose of God to serve his own selfish goals, and the result was catastrophic. Have you confused God's will with your goals?

Perfect Identity

Jesus is the only example of someone who was perfectly rooted in His own identity, which is why we can look to Him as our example. Jesus knew who He was. He wasn't confused about His personhood or His purpose. When we pay attention to this—to how Jesus acted and reacted, where He traveled and what He said—we get a picture of what it looks like to have a strong sense of self, rooted in Christ.

When we look at the life of Jesus, we see that He wasn't a slave to the crowd. People around Him attempted to influence Him with their opinions, and tried to pressure Him to do certain things in certain ways, but He didn't bend to their whims, no matter how loudly they spoke. From my experience, the loudest voices aren't always the most important ones. Jesus knew His plan and His purpose and stuck with them. He understood, at the end of the day, that He answered to the Father.

Jesus said things He knew would make Him unpopular. Raised in a culture familiar with the terrors of child sacrifice, and leery of the cannibalistic rituals of the pagan religions in ancient Mesopotamia, He knew that Jews operated under strict rules about food sources. The notion of eating a person and drinking blood offended the religious mind and broke the sacrificial and Levitical law. Still, Jesus, knowing what He was about to say, chose to say it anyway:

> "For my flesh is true food, and my blood is true drink. He who eats my flesh and drinks my blood abides in Me, and I in him. As the living Father sent Me, and I live because of the Father, so he who eats Me, he also will live because of Me." (John 6:55–57, ESV)

Did you catch this? Jesus revealed a piece of His identity only He could understand, as He was about to die on the cross and give up His body and blood for humanity. He made Himself vulnerable enough to *be Himself* regardless of how misunderstood He would be. He referenced the Father, the source of His identity, the One who spoke identity over Him when He came up out of the water after baptism. "This is my Son, whom I love; with him I am well pleased" (Matt. 3:17). Yet He said it in a way He knew would be offensive to those who were listening.

This passage goes on to say that, at this point, many of His disciples departed. Some of His friends left Him. People began to doubt Him. Still, Jesus stood His ground. He didn't look to the crowd to tell Him who He was. He looked to the Father.

When the crowd leaves, may this never change who we are.

What if Jesus had allowed selfish motives or a desire to secure a position to override His ultimate calling? Can you imagine if He had bent to the Pharisees who urged Him not to heal on the Sabbath? What if He had simply walked the other direction when He saw people selling sacrifices for absurd prices in the temple? I don't know about you, but I'm so grateful Jesus didn't become a slave to the crowd. We can learn a lot from Him.

> Praise God that Jesus was secure in His identity. Because of this, He was also able to give others the gift of identity.

It's so easy for us to allow reputation or image management to replace or override our true identities. But this is one of the most destructive things we can do, and I think it's also one of the most difficult challenges of our time. With the rise of social media and individual importance, it can be so easy to get sidetracked by what other people think of us, how we look from the outside, and how many followers or fans we have. But Scripture says God doesn't care what we look like from the outside. Instead, He cares what's in our hearts.

A good test of identity is whether or not our convictions or opinion change simply based on who is in the room with us. If we change based on who is around, our identity is fluid. Jesus can make it solid. Making decisions based on preserving our reputation is an indicator we're dead inside. Consider your own daily decisions. How many are made with an honest reflection of who you are in Jesus—and how many are made with a calculation of what others might think? A lack of identity can sneak up on us and is one of the most dangerous traps in the world.

Praise God that Jesus was secure in His identity. Because of this, He was also able to give others the gift of identity. Consider the beautiful story from Mark 5 where Jesus healed the woman who had been bleeding for twelve years. Scripture says she *pressed through* the crowd to get to Jesus. At the time, probably about 4,000 people were in the crowd—peasants, beggars, priests, and seekers—in Jerusalem. This woman didn't want to speak with any of those priests. She wanted to be in the presence of Jesus. She wanted to speak with *Him*. It makes me wonder if she had an innate sense that Jesus could give her more than physical healing—that He could help her untangle her identity.

This woman had been sick for twelve years. She'd been bleeding for all that time, which had implications beyond her physical health. First, she would have been considered unclean, which means she would have been segregated from the rest of her community. Her husband may or may not have left her. Scripture doesn't give us these details. But based on culture and historical norms, we can guess she was extremely lonely. Scholars predict she was probably shrunken from old age and her illness. My guess is she was a walking skeleton, alone and slowly dying. Still, she pushed her way through the crowd. That's how desperate she was to get to Jesus.

Additionally, this woman had given everything she had in a desperate attempt to solve the problem—and still, she was sick. Is there a problem in your life you've given all of your resources and energy to solve but you just can't fix? Maybe it's an addiction of some kind or maybe you're unemployed and can't find work.

Maybe you have an illness no one can diagnose. Or maybe you have a child who has made decisions you disagree with, and they're suffering the consequences.

It's not that you're lazy or not trying. It's just that life is complicated and there are no easy solutions. When this woman finally reached Jesus in the middle of the crowd, she reached out to touch His cloak. She was convinced—*If I can only touch His coat, I'll be healed.*

Scripture says that as soon as she touched Him, Jesus realized power had left Him. He turned to her. And this, to me, is the most amazing part of the story. He said to her, "Daughter, your faith has made you well." The words He used are extremely important. Let's look at the Greek. The Greek word He used for "daughter" is a term of endearment. Yes, He had healed her physically. The Bible says her flow of bleeding stopped. But if you ask me, the healing was not the real miracle here. The real miracle was that Jesus called her "daughter." Now she had an identity. Before dealing with her issue or illness, He dealt with her identity.

The woman came to Jesus to treat an issue. We all do this: "Jesus, will you heal my mom from cancer?" "Jesus, will you help me overcome my bad habit?" "Jesus, will you help me find peace for such-and-such decision?" "Jesus, we need a hundred dollars." Jesus cares about our issues. But more than our issues, Jesus cares about us. When Jesus approached Legion, when He approached this woman, when He approaches us, the first thing He says—the most important thing to Him is, "What is your name?" He uses a term of endearment—"daughter."

When you encounter Jesus, you get identity. And when you have identity, you are able to give the gift of identity to others. It only makes sense—since we are made in the image of Christ, if we live in our true identity, others are able to find their place and purpose as well.

Jesus' ability to give identity is profound. In fact, it's so profound that it doesn't just apply to people. It applies to situations, to motives, and to circumstances as well. Where there is no Jesus, there is no identity. Where there is no identity, there is confusion, anxiety, and fear. Jesus has the ability to dissect a moment to the lowest common denominator and bring forward identity. With that, He brings joy, peace, and love. Jesus healed the man possessed by the legion of demons in Mark 5, and the man was restored and clothed. Literally, Scripture says, "He was dressed and in his right mind." Identity—coming back to himself—had happened.

Do you know who you are in Jesus? Are you willing to lay down who you want to be and allow Him to show you who you are? Will you run from across the shore, like the man possessed by Legion? Will you press through the crowd like this bleeding woman?

How Do I Know If I Know Who I Am?

When we follow the way of Jesus rather than chase our own selfish ambitions, we don't have to wonder about our identity anymore. We don't perform for it, nor do we strive to have it. Identify is gifted to us, the same way it was gifted to the man tormented by 6,000 demons and to the bleeding woman. Identity is a byproduct of encountering Jesus. The byproduct of identity is joy and peace. You'll know when you find your identity—because when you know your identity, you find peace.

In Genesis 3, when the serpent tempted Eve to eat the fruit from the Tree of Knowledge of Good and Evil, we see that an original lie was embedded inside the original sin. The serpent asked, "Did God really say . . . ?" In other words, can God be trusted? Is God who He says He is? Then the serpent said, "For God knows . . . you will be like God" (v. 5). In other words: You aren't good enough the way you are. Satan's original lie said that God wasn't who He said He was, and you aren't who He says you are.

Identity is the cure for these lies, and identity is revealed when we meet Jesus. As we grow in our relationship with Him— as we slow down and listen to His voice, as we learn to turn and see, as we discover just how sacred the ground is we walk on each day—we also grow in understanding who He made us to be.

The impact of the man known as Legion didn't end in Luke 8. In the latter part of Mark 6, we read that Jesus traveled back to the region where He first encountered Legion. The reception on this second visit was significantly different. Where the people had previously begged Jesus to leave (Luke 8:34), they now lined up for Him to heal their sick. Why the change? After Jesus left the area, this man known as Legion continued the conversation in the region. We don't know his given name, but we do know the effects of his life after meeting Jesus. We know he spread the news of what Jesus said to him and did for him. Some of eternity's most profound moments go unannounced here on earth. A man whose identity was restored by Jesus brought the kingdom to earth for many.

We are part of a greater story, aren't we? This story isn't ours alone. It's God's, and He declares the end from the beginning. Regardless of what path we find ourselves on, it's paved in His righteousness. We have nothing to fear. He remains profoundly with us, whether we realize it or not. His love knows no bounds. His comfort is within reach.

Will you press through the crowd? Will you run to the shore to greet Him?

CHAPTER SIX

How Close Is Close Enough?

Are you stewarding life's unannounced moments?

I'm not supposed to be here. When I look back on the story I've lived, I'm amazed I'm still alive. I should have died at least a dozen times. Although none of those close calls took my life, I thought many times about taking it myself. When I look back now, I cringe at the opportunities for a true encounter with Jesus that I let slip through the cracks. I know now how precious each moment is when Jesus reveals Himself to us.

Opportunities rarely repeat themselves, and by no means do they last forever. This is true about any opportunity—whether it's for a job, to date or marry a certain person, to move to another place, or to encounter Jesus. We never know what opportunity will be our last one. We have to assume this chance is our last one. Well-known pastor Steve Hill popularized this saying: "The opportunity of a lifetime must be seized within the lifetime of the opportunity."[1] I couldn't agree more.

Even as I sit here writing this book—or as you sit wherever you are reading it—neither of us can assume we'll be alive tomorrow, or even long enough to finish writing or reading it. We must each assume this moment is our last. The urgency of that feeling drives us to seize opportunities because we never know if that opportunity will be in front of us again.

Despite your searching, Jesus is near. The bush is burning, even in the midst of the unannounced moments of life—the raging storms, the barren desert. As you seek to work out your identity, the ground where you tread is sacred. Heaven is closing in all around you. The question is: Will you reach out and touch it? Will you miss this one, sacred, beautiful opportunity?

A Blind Man Teaches Us to See

There's a story in Mark 10:40–52 that grabs my attention every time I read it because it demonstrates the importance of a moment. In this passage, a blind man sat outside the gates of Jericho, the city where the walls had supernaturally fallen hundreds of years earlier (Josh. 6). The story of this battle had been handed down, generation after generation, as evidence of God's sovereign hand. Nothing was impossible for Him. But many people had forgotten. Those who walked the course of the city on a day-to-day basis could reach out and touch the ruins—yet many of them missed their significance. A city of broken walls had become a city of broken people. This blind beggar was one of many.

For a moment, put yourself in the blind man's shoes. You find yourself immersed in the tangible evidence that God is real, that He can perform miracles—and yet you're blind. Many of us can relate. We know He's among us and we believe He can do all things; yet, our circumstances seem to tell a different story. We know He's powerful, but we don't see His power in our lives. For anyone who has stood in this position, it's not hard to imagine the humiliation this man must have felt—standing on the streets, begging for loose change.

> Desperation calls us to press through ridicule and accusation from those around us, for the hope of a single encounter with the Savior.

Typically, those who couldn't work stood at the gates of the city where there would be a lot of foot traffic, so they could ask for coins from passersby. This was likely the daily routine for this man. But on this particular day, he heard Jesus was coming. So, desperate for a healing touch, he began calling out for Him.

Obviously, the blind man couldn't see when Jesus passed by. He had never met Jesus, so he wouldn't know the sound of His voice or have any other way to identify Him. As he called out to Jesus, I can only assume he did so repeatedly, over and over again. Scripture even says, "The crowd rebuked him," asking him to stop crying out. But the man wouldn't stop.

Imagine the desperation. Or perhaps you don't have to imagine because you've felt it yourself. Desperation calls us to press through ridicule and accusation from those around us, for the hope of a single encounter with the Savior.

Some people thought this beggar was drawing too much attention to himself. Others felt he was disturbing the peace. Even a few thought he was distracting Jesus from something more important. Still, the beggar continued to cry out. Sometimes, our willingness to be misunderstood by those around us becomes our tipping point for an encounter with the divine. If we are to be criticized or accused of anything, let it be that we refuse to miss a moment when Jesus is present.

The blind beggar wasn't swayed by the crowd, and fortunately, Jesus wasn't either. Jesus never is. He is swayed, however, by the cries of those who reach out to Him. Can you change God's mind? Scripture is clear that God's mind is not changed—however His heart is influenced. Whenever we mention His name—whether we're on the Jericho road, at a coffee shop, sitting in class, or in the car—He always answers our call. This is exactly what happened that day when a blind man in Jericho cried out.

He's always more concerned about our spiritual needs than our physical ones. He always exceeds our expectations, when we let Him.

There are a few things to note about this story. First, if we look closely, we can see this man didn't just call out for Jesus. He called out for the "Son of David," a reference to the fact that Jesus was the Messiah. Not only was the man's cry a desperate plea for help—it was also an emphatic declaration of who Jesus was.

What incredible courage and conviction this man had! We can learn a lot from him. He's the blind man who teaches all of us to truly see.

Eventually, Jesus did pass by, and the man caught His attention. This is the part of the story I really love. Jesus stopped and listened to him. Then Jesus asked, "What do you want me to do for you?" The man replied: "Rabbi, I want to see." The Greek word for sight here is *ophthalmoi*—meaning physical sight. But Scripture records that Jesus gave the man *ommata*, a word Plato used poetically to describe the eyes of the soul: spiritual sight. The man asked for physical healing, and Jesus responded in a spiritual way.

Sometimes, when we encounter Jesus, we think we want Him to meet a physical need, but He chooses to respond by meeting a spiritual one. This is the second thing I think is important to note about this story. Even when Jesus gives us a blank check—"what can I do for you?"—the greatest thing we desire is still nothing compared to what He wants to offer. He's always more concerned about our spiritual needs than our physical ones. He always exceeds our expectations, when we let Him.

Finally, I can't help but wonder what would have happened if he had been too ashamed, or too uncomfortable, to cry out to Jesus that day. What if he had waited until he thought he heard Jesus, or until someone told him Jesus was passing by? Would he have missed Jesus altogether? Would he have gone his entire life without ever getting his sight back? Would he have stayed spiritually blind? Perhaps. Based on Scripture, we know that Jesus never passed this way again. Some opportunities are only presented to us once. If we don't seize them, we won't ever be able to. They will be lost forever.

Am I Going to Die?

It was late in the afternoon. School was out. Rumor had it a party was going on and the beer was free. So I did the only thing I could think to do—drove to meet my friends and kick off the weekend. It was rush hour traffic, and I was in a car with three other guys. As we drove down the road, a green van pulled up next to us and launched a beer can onto our hood.

For a moment, time stood still. That is, until the driver of our car realized what had happened and proceeded to communicate his anger to the other driver—using words and actions better left unwritten. Words went back and forth until finally, the green van sideswiped our car; and memories of the infamous TV show, *The A-Team,* flooded my mind. In what felt like a scene out of a movie, the van continued to bump into our little Volkswagen. Side dented, paint chipped—cue our (or at least my) deep concern.

"Those guys are drunk!" I yelled to my friends. "Somebody's 'gonna get killed if we don't get out of here!"

Speeding up to avoid another collision, we turned abruptly down a side street. The green van slammed on its brakes, and the tires smoked and squealed behind us. My friend knew we only had a limited time to get away before the van caught up to us, so he picked up the pace even more. I remember looking at the speedometer and seeing it hit the 100 mph mark—just before we ran a stop sign. Moments later, we slammed into a car that had been at a complete stop and spun around.

What happened next is only clear to me because of what people have told me. Eye-witnesses recounted that my body was thrown through the trunk of the car, out the backside and down the street, where I hit my head on a telephone pole. The first thing I remember thinking when I woke up was, *If I die, I'm going to go to hell.*

When I looked up, I saw a familiar face. It was my stepdad's friend. They played softball together. I remember thinking he looked worried and then immediately feeling around in my mouth with my tongue wondering, *where are my teeth?* I thought they had been knocked out of my mouth as I tasted blood—or, better said, as I drank it. Turns out, my teeth weren't knocked out at all. Instead, my jaw was broken and shoved into my head. I was banged up pretty bad.

"Am I going to die?" I asked.

"You're pretty beat up," was all he said. Then he started to cry.

The paramedics rushed me to the hospital and saved my life. My jaw had to be wired shut for it to heal, which meant only a liquid diet for several weeks. The recreational drugs that were part of my regimen were completely out of the question. The doctor spoke with me sternly and warned me that if I did drugs in my condition, I would die. So, I determined to quit.

For weeks, I stayed clean. I drank food and regained my strength in the hospital. My family came to be with me. I even had a visit from the girl who had heard God tell her in her heart to pray for me a few years earlier. But a lot of "friends" I'd spent the weekends partying with were absent. They didn't call and few, if any, came by. It wasn't until I got out of the hospital that I heard anything from those supposed "friends," wondering when I'd be well enough to come party again.

There's nothing lonelier than realizing the people you were supposed to "belong" to don't really want you after all. Jesus understands. He was despised and rejected by those who were supposed to be closest to Him. He's the One we can rely on. Always—even when we don't understand.

My life has been filled with close calls like this. Seriously, I could go on for hours. I'm amazed God never gave up on me, amazed at how many chances He gave me to trust in Him. By the grace of God, I'm here. But how do we know what chance will be our last one? How can we be certain this chance—the one right in front of us—won't be our last opportunity to encounter Jesus.

A Girl and a Letter

One Wednesday after youth group, the young woman who listened to God and prayed for me—the one who came to visit me in the hospital—was doing her Sunday school homework. She was going through her prayer list and praying for people. That's when she stumbled across my name. She remembered the questions I had asked her in eighth grade about God and how, at the time, she wasn't interested in finding the answers. Back then, she hadn't realized how important they were. In that moment, however, she decided to write me a letter.

She sat down to write out the words and put her soul on paper. Her goal wasn't to convince or coerce but to be honest about how her heart had changed. Once she felt she had put everything on the paper, she put it in an envelope, sealed it, and put it in her purse, where it stayed for a few weeks.

At first, she wasn't going to send it. *It was weird to send a letter like that, wasn't it?* We were friends, or acquaintances at least. She could pick up the phone and call. Should she really put the letter in the mail? Nevertheless, one day as she was walking around the mall, something happened. That same subtle impression she had in eighth grade came to her again, *Mail the letter.* So she did. Not willing to miss a moment or an opportunity, she slipped the letter into the blue mailbox at Southridge Mall—a temporary resting place for words that would alter my life forever.

Have you ever thought how our opportunities to encounter Jesus—or to awake to the realities of heaven—might be limited? For the most part, we don't live our day-to-day lives like this. We wake up in the morning and think how to make it through the day. We think about getting a cup of coffee and what time we have to leave to make it to the office in time. We think about what we're going to wear that day and—do I need a shirt ironed? We think about breakfast or a deadline.

No matter how you spend your moments, are you considering that this moment will never come again? Are you stewarding your moments in ways that recognize how precious they are, that this moment might be all you have?

> Are you stewarding your moments in ways that recognize how precious they are, that this moment might be all you have?

I don't mean this in a cheesy way. We've all heard the youth pastor talk about what would happen if you stepped off the sidewalk and were hit by a bus. But rather than thinking about where you would go if you were hit by a bus, I'm asking you to consider how each moment in your life is a chance to encounter the true and living God. Each moment is an opportunity to experience His grace, His love, and His transforming power. The bush always burns, and the ground is always sacred. When we awake to this reality, we find certain peace in the midst of our storms. We come to know Him and ourselves more fully. He speaks life into our dead places.

When we begin to think about Jesus like this, we don't need scare tactics like, "Where will you go when you die?" With each passing moment—each unique and irreplaceable second—Jesus is begging you to experience the fullness of His love. With that in mind, you don't want to miss it, do you?

If you have memories of moments missed, don't allow the noise of the crowd to prevent you from calling out to Jesus. You don't need an explanation for your condition. You only need to know His name. Don't let guilt or shame frustrate the conversation He's trying to have with you. Allow conviction to penetrate. Let Him call you daughter or son. He speaks your name. His mercies are new every morning.

Your Moment

Think about a moment in your life when an opportunity was right in front of you. Maybe it was a new job or a chance to say yes to a proposal. Or maybe it was an opportunity to turn from a destructive relationship, habit, or addiction. You were standing there, looking into the face of the person you loved or looking at an acceptance letter or email feeling the weight of this moment of decision. No matter what the decision was, decisions have expiration dates. Again, the opportunity of a lifetime must be seized during the lifetime of the opportunity.

If it's a new job you're waiting to accept, you might have until Friday to decide. If it's a proposal, typically you must decide in that moment. Even as you move through the day, your opportunity to experience certain things or see certain people is limited. Today only happens once. *Tomorrow* is a word found only on a fool's calendar. So when will your last opportunity be to have an encounter with Jesus or come to know Him in a more profound way? Nobody knows. We do know that time is short, and there is no guarantee of another opportunity. The blind man in Mark 10 teaches us not only how to seize the day but to see (spiritually) the day. Most of us don't realize this kind of urgency until we've lived it.

The kind of life you're waiting for—a deep life of meaning and fulfillment, full of love and joy—can be found at the place where all these things intersect: an encounter with Jesus, a strong identity, an abandonment of self, an understanding of the urgent, embracing the invitation, a seized opportunity, and a stewarded moment. These are the ingredients of a strong faith.

Jesus can rewrite anyone's story. If He can rewrite mine (from drug addict and dark soul to son of the King, husband, dad, pastor, author, and speaker), He can rewrite yours. By the way, everyone needs Jesus to rewrite their story. He didn't come to earth to make non-Christians become Christians. He didn't come to make bad people good. He came because we're dead in sin and lost without Him. He came to rewrite our story—something we can't do ourselves, regardless of how good our deeds are.

Do we need good deeds? Absolutely! We should all have fruit growing on our trees. But for this to happen, we have to let go of the religious acts that distract us from Him. We have to abandon self-promotion and selfish ambition and wake up to the profound nature of Jesus. We must slow down enough to notice the quiet acts of God happening all around us. The bush is always burning. The ground is always sacred.

I said in the beginning of this chapter that I'm not supposed to be here, but I take that back. I *am* supposed to be here, and so are you. God has ordered every moment of our lives. He directs our every step. His response is never reactive. He proactively shapes history by folding our lives into His plan (Acts 4:28). He is calling. Right now, He offers an opportunity. He wants to rewrite your story. This is your moment. Are you listening?

CHAPTER SEVEN

Questions About God

Will you allow His voice to be your answer?

B y fall of 1994, things in my life were pretty good, depending on your definition of the word *good*. I was memorizing the satanic Bible, getting good grades, had money in my pocket, and was feeling pretty good about myself and my life. There had been a lot of noise in my life around the God conversation. I learned some things from catechism classes, as well as from others who provided books on Buddhism and urged me to see Jesus as a philosopher and teacher, but not as God.

Still, I never stopped asking questions about God.

My friend and I would smoke weed in the park, and he would talk to me about the story of the man possessed by 6,000 demons that identified themselves as "Legion." I remember how he opened his black Bible and read out of Mark 5 about this tormented soul. He was fascinated with demon possession, so we would read from Mark and speculate about how many demons exactly were trapped inside the man.

There was also a guy in my physics class who went to church. I would show up to class, tripping on acid, and strike up a conversation with him, asking him to tell me what he knew about God. One day he told me he was "saving himself for marriage," and I had never heard of such a thing. I had no idea what that even meant, but I was fascinated.

My friend Paul's mom was also a Christian. I perceived her as the Bible-thumping, voice-raising, "powers of hell" kind of Christian. Sometimes we would go over to Paul's house, and she would make us the best spaghetti. The only requirement was that we stay and listen to her read Scripture and talk about God. She would hold her cigarette in one hand and her big red Bible in the other, preaching to us the truths about heaven, hell, and how Jesus was the only true God. It was hard to take her seriously, to be honest, but we kept going back. The spaghetti was just that good.

Perhaps the most confusing part about all of this was trying to balance my upbringing with the things I was learning about God. In our family it was generally understood that preachers were sleazy—all they wanted was your money. And I found my childhood filled with bitterness, regret, fear, and anger difficult to reconcile with the existence of a good God. When it comes to our questions about God, it's easy to get lost in the sea of voices and to let them drown out the one voice we really need to hear.

It doesn't matter whether you're new to Jesus, you've been a Christian your whole life, or you've never had an authentic encounter with Him—many voices in this world vie for your

CHAPTER SEVEN: QUESTIONS ABOUT GOD

attention. More voices now than ever. There are televangelists and street-corner preachers. There are door-to-door missionaries and online personalities. There are books, movies, television, and music—all trying to tell you something different about God. How do we sift through all the noise to hear from the One who truly has the answers?

Church

The first place we usually go when we want to know about God is church. Or, at least that's what I did that year. I grabbed my friend Paul, who I would always get drunk and high with, and convinced him to come with me to the only church we knew about, the one my physics partner attended. Sunday came— which also happened to be Super Bowl Sunday—and Paul begrudgingly joined me for the service, complaining the whole way about missing the game. Missing the Super Bowl was a big deal for me, too. I gave up the nacho buffet and Little Smokies simmering in Mom's Crock-Pot for a church service. There was no logical reason why I was even going. Something inside me compelled me. I looked for answers everywhere I could.

The first thing I saw when I walked through the front doors of that church was people raising their hands and clapping, swaying and singing at the top of their lungs. On top of that, when the preacher spoke he yelled and spit and a giant vein popped out of his forehead. This was like nothing I had seen at the Catholic church. To be honest, I wasn't sure what to do with it. I honestly thought everyone was nuts. I felt uncomfortable. Yet at the same time, I assumed everyone in the room had their act together and was an outstanding moral person. I figured if they knew the things I had done, I wouldn't be welcome there.

Paul and I found our seats and settled in. A middle-aged couple stood behind us. I acknowledged them with a slight nod and then turned to the front of the room where the pastor was speaking. At one point during the service, the man I'd acknowledged stood up and began shouting in a language I didn't understand. I recognized this as speaking in tongues. It reminded me of the demonic tongues I had experienced in the spiritual realm through other avenues.

> If you ask me, we often go to church seeking answers the church can't give.

I remember thinking it was weird that the preacher opened up a black leather-bound book and assumed it was relevant for every one of us in the room. I honestly remember thinking, *How does he know that a con artist didn't make up the Bible on a rural farm in Pennsylvania?* Random, I know. I had no idea what the preacher was saying. I didn't understand why everyone was wearing a suit; after all, my Grateful Dead T-shirt had a marijuana leaf on it. I slipped in and slipped out. I'm not sure if any of those people noticed, but Jesus did.

Needless to say, I left church that day without feeling much closer to the answers I sought. If anything, I had more questions. Why was worshipping God any different, really, than reading Nietzsche, studying Siddhartha, or talking to an unknown spirit while playing football with friends at Ewing Park? What made church so different from the Ouija board experiences or the séances I'd had? How was the "experience" I'd had at church different from smoking weed and talking about the Legion story in the car?

If you ask me, we often go to church seeking answers the church can't give. Church can give us some answers, of course, but for the most part, the church is a community of people who choose to do life together, worship God together, and come together to demonstrate how beautiful Christ is. Even those who encountered Jesus in the Scriptures didn't always get the answers they wanted. In fact, they often got more questions.

What You Know Can Hurt You

There's a story in Scripture about a man—a Pharisee—who came to Jesus with some questions. The Pharisees were a group of people committed to maintaining the purity of the Jewish religion. The word *Pharisee* means "separate one." Their job was to stay pure and not allow anyone to taint them, regardless of persecution. And while they started out as a blessing to the Hebrew people, over time they lost sight of their identity and, therefore, lost sight of what mattered. Many of the Pharisees had allowed what they thought they knew about God to prevent them from seeing when God was right in front of them.

One such Pharisee was Nicodemus. One day, he came to Jesus and said, "Rabbi, we know you are a teacher who has come from God. For no one could perform the signs you are doing if God were not with Him" (John 3:2). Notice that, like Judas, Nicodemus called Jesus "good teacher" but also acknowledged that Jesus had come from God. You can tell Nicodemus was conflicted.

In verse 3, Jesus responded, "Very truly, I tell you, no one can see the kingdom of God unless they are born again."

Jesus' response is interesting for a couple of reasons. First, He didn't answer the question. Nicodemus wanted to know who Jesus was, and Jesus responded by talking about the kingdom of heaven. Second, this is the first time in the New Testament that Jesus talked about being born again—a concept that Nicodemus, for obvious reasons, had a hard time wrapping his brain around. A confused Nicodemus asked Jesus, "How can a man be born when he is old? Can he enter a second time into his mother's womb and be born?" He came to Jesus with a question and left with more questions.

The most interesting thing about this encounter is this: What Nicodemus already knew prevented him from understanding what Jesus tried to tell him. In other words, because he already understood what it meant to be born, he had a difficult time understanding what it meant to be born *again*. I can just imagine him thinking through the logistics of this. Meanwhile, Jesus said to him (and to us), that the way things work on earth is not the same way they work in the kingdom of heaven.

Nicodemus was steeped in religious training. He had acquired immense knowledge from religious and rabbinical writings. Yet when he looked at the very object of his lifelong journey and pursuit of knowledge, he didn't recognize

> Understanding God isn't about getting answers to all our questions. It's about slowing down and getting quiet enough to listen.

it. Sometimes, like Nicodemus, what we *think* we know about Jesus prevents us from truly *knowing* Him. Ironically, our craving to know God can get in the way of knowing God.

At some point, we have to forget the idea that we shouldn't ask questions. It's normal to have questions about God, eternity, and how this whole story is playing out on earth. Even the disciples—those who walked with Jesus and knew Him best— had questions. Countless times in Scripture, the disciples asked Jesus questions, and His response only elicited more questions. Questions often tell us more than answers do. Understanding God isn't about getting answers to all our questions. It's about slowing down and getting quiet enough to listen.

One Voice

In Exodus 2, we find a man who had stopped asking questions. Moses, raised in affluence, was destined to receive immense wealth and power. He was the stepson of Pharaoh. He felt the purpose of God strongly in his life—to free the Hebrews from slavery. But due to a few mistakes—his impatience, his unwillingness to wait on God, and perhaps his inability to hear God's voice clearly—he took matters into his own hands and murdered an Egyptian. This event sent him wandering into the desert for forty years.

In the desert, Moses started a family and began his career. By the time we get to chapter 3, it's apparent he had stopped asking questions. He had settled down. He had decided it was too risky to ask questions. He remembered the last time he had tried to hear from God and how he had ruined everything. He had heard wrongly. He had acted wrongly. So Moses decided to give up. There's no evidence, at this point, that Moses was seeking to engage God anymore. Yet this is the very moment God chose to show up in a miraculous way—a burning bush. God answered Moses, who hadn't even asked a question. Or, more accurately, Moses turned and saw the answer that had been there all along.

Jesus' voice isn't necessarily the loudest voice in the room, but it's the most important. Author Henri Nouwen said, "There was a time when silence was normal and a lot of racket disturbed us. But today, noise is the normal fare, and silence has become the real disturbance."[1] Likewise, psychology professor Ester Buchholz says, "Others inspire us, information feeds us, practice improves our performance, but we need quiet time to figure things out, to emerge with new discoveries, to unearth original answers."[2] What if what we need most to hear the Lord's voice is just a little bit of silence?

In my life, the first sign I was beginning to hear God's voice above all the noise was the guilt I began to feel every time I got high. I would go to the park with my friends, like usual, or sneak back to my room; but every time I got drunk or did drugs, I got a nagging feeling in my gut—that this wasn't how it was supposed to be. I was doing something wrong. I didn't have a moral compass or faith-based upbringing to tell me it was wrong, but God's voice often breaks quietly and subtly through our conscience.

One typical Sunday afternoon, I went to a park with some friends to hang out and do drugs. There was enough crystal meth for a few of us, so we did what was there and followed it up with alcohol and marijuana. Paul brought his Bible, as usual, and read the story of Legion from Mark 5. We read and talked and hung out for several hours, then I went back home and shut myself in my room for the night to let my high wear off.

The effects of the drugs kept me from eating or sleeping that night, which was fairly typical. I lay awake, wondering again about God. I wanted to know the *truth*. Who was God, and what did He want from me? What was I missing? I lay awake for several hours, wrestling and questioning and wondering—until finally it felt as if Truth came to *me*. Truth was not an idea or an abstract philosophical concept. Truth was a person. Truth is a person.

> Jesus' voice isn't necessarily the loudest voice in the room, but it's the most important.

I felt a tangible love fill my bedroom. I was sober now and clear-headed enough to know exactly what was happening. I knew, beyond a shadow of a doubt, the presence of a loving God had entered my room. It was the quietest voice I had ever heard—in fact, there was no sound at all—but it was also the most convincing.

All the questions I'd ever had seemed to be answered in that moment. Not with words, but with the touch of the Savior. I started to weep. When Love comes over you, you can't help but feel overwhelmed with joy—and even sadness for how long you've lived without it. I felt humbled and awed—free of any condemnation, rage, or rejection from Jesus. I felt only pure, unconditional love. Tears coursed down my face as I whispered, "You are who You say You are."

It's amazing how when we tune out the voices of those around us, we finally hear the one Voice that matters. It's amazing how something that seems so complicated can, in a moment, become so simple. No matter how far away from God you perceive yourself to be, the bush always burns and the ground is always sacred.

That night changed everything for me. The following morning, I woke up and went to school like usual. But as I moved through my day, I thought about what had happened the night before. Finally, I had found a love that could satisfy all my questions. When Love comes, answers are no longer as necessary. I couldn't wait to get home to continue the conversation with Jesus.

Strangely enough, it never dawned on me that I could talk to Him anywhere and anytime. All I knew was I had met Him in my bedroom that night, and I longed to be in His presence again— the same way the young girl who prayed for me had felt when she encountered the love of Christ in her Bible study.

That day, in physics class, I asked Gavin if I could go to church with him the next time he went. I had been to church before, but I knew this time would be different. I needed to do that thing where you go to the front and pray with a pastor. I didn't even know what it was—but I knew I needed to do it. Gavin told me I could come with him on Wednesday night, and I agreed. It was only two days away, but I waited for Wednesday with great anticipation.

That night in my bedroom, Jesus had reached out to me in a miraculous way, but I still had a part to play. It reminds me of the time when Jesus raised Lazarus from the dead in John 11:38–44. Jesus asked Lazarus' sisters, Mary and Martha, and the other people there to move the stone away from Lazarus' tomb. Jesus could easily have done this Himself. He was about to raise a dead man from the grave, after all! So why ask someone to move a large rock when He could easily do it with a breath of air or a spoken word? Because people could move the stone, but they couldn't raise the dead. I like what author Joyce Meyer says, "God won't do for you what you can do yourself. You must do what you can do, and then trust God to do what you can't."[3]

After Lazarus rose from the dead, he was completely alive yet still wrapped in grave clothes. Jesus asked those nearby to unwrap Lazarus. Again, Jesus called them to action. Quite possibly, the most tragic state of existence is to be alive, awake and free, yet still wrapped in bondage, unable to enjoy freedom. After Jesus raises us from our slumber, the next step is up to us. Will we continue to question Him when He has already provided the answer? Or will we unwrap ourselves from the grave clothes that entangle us? Will we turn and see?

Hearing Jesus Out

Let's look at Nicodemus again. We see a man who had questions about God but wasn't sure Jesus was who He claimed to be. When we look forward in the story of Nicodemus, we see another side of this man—a man who wanted to hear Jesus out.

The story picks up in John 7. Several religious leaders had gathered to discuss what to do about Jesus. They had overheard people talking about Jesus and speculating about who He was. The Pharisees were beginning to see Him as a threat to their power and what they wanted to accomplish in Judea. So rather than let things play out and risk losing their power, they sent the temple guards to arrest Jesus. But the guards soon returned without Jesus.

"Why didn't you bring Him in?" the Pharisees asked.

The guards replied, "No one ever spoke the way He does."

I can only imagine how the religious leaders must have stared blankly at the guards. These men went out with one goal in mind—to arrest Jesus—yet when they showed up on the scene, they got distracted from their goal (their *job*) because they were so taken by what Jesus said. Ultimately, they returned to the temple, telling the religious leaders (their bosses), "We just couldn't bring ourselves to arrest Him." The guards heard and felt the same loving voice I did in my bedroom that night—the same loving voice I continue to hear today.

> How often do we dismiss Jesus before we've really listened to Him?

As the religious leaders argued about what to do, Nicodemus interceded. This is the same man who called Jesus "rabbi" a few chapters earlier. It's the same man who doubted when Jesus tried to explain being born again. The same man whose "knowledge" of God prevented Him from realizing God was standing right in front of him. But notice what happened. Nicodemus said, "Does our law condemn a man without first hearing him to find out what he has been doing?" In other words, before we accuse Him, *maybe we should hear Him out.*

This was perhaps as shocking to the religious leaders as the temple guards showing up without Jesus. Nicodemus risked his reputation, his dignity, and possibly even his life to urge the men who would ultimately kill Jesus to stop for a minute and listen to the One who could provide all the answers they needed.

How often do we dismiss Jesus before we've really listened to Him? Perhaps we've listened to what other people are saying about Him, but we haven't actually listened *to* Him. Too often we look at what His followers are doing, and we get a bad taste in our mouths. But we haven't really cleared out the noise and listened directly to Him. Are we following Jesus or Christianity?

Perhaps you think you've already heard Jesus out. You went to church or you talked to a Christian, but you didn't like what you heard or you still have questions. God has the answers. Or a better way to say it is this: God is the answer *and* He is the question. Truth isn't an idea; it's a person.

Getting to the Truth

Part of the problem is that most of us *think* we're hungry for truth, but we're really hungry for comfort. Truth offends us. It provokes us. Ultimately, it transforms us, and that process can be uncomfortable. The real truth is: If we're willing to sincerely start a conversation with God, we'll receive the answers we need. We don't need to worry about a false God coming. We don't need to obsess over the answers. Remember, truth isn't an idea; He's a person. According to Hebrews 13:8, He's the same "yesterday, today, and forever." The truth found in Jesus is ancient yet completely relevant to us today.

We see this demonstrated beautifully in John 4, where Jesus had a conversation with a woman who, by all appearances, didn't know God. This wasn't the kind of woman you would find in today's churches. In fact, you'd more likely find her at the local strip club. Still, Jesus met her and struck up a conversation (you can imagine how controversial this was).

As Jesus returned from a wave of baptisms in Judea, He passed through Samaria. Interestingly, He didn't *have* to go that way. In fact, most Jewish men would have taken the longer route to bypass Samaritan land, considered to be unclean. But Jesus passed right through Samaria, and even rested there in the middle of the day. He found a woman drawing water from a well.

The fact that she was drawing water from the well in the middle of the day tells us something. Because of the heat in this region, most people ventured to the well in the morning or in the evening—it was a central gathering place, a place to see familiar faces and swap stories. This woman wasn't interested in seeing any familiar faces. She was likely the story being swapped. This is our first indication she had something to hide.

The second is that Jesus quickly and simply stated what she was hiding. He initiated a conversation with her and, in minutes, aired her dirty laundry: "The fact is, you have had five husbands, and the man you now have is not your husband." I imagine, at this point, the woman froze. She had been found out.

The interesting thing is she didn't deny what He said. She didn't defend it or push back. She didn't try to argue for her own truth. She saw the truth because Truth was standing right in front of her. Because she wanted to know the truth, she was able to receive the truth. Truth is filtered through the desires of our hearts. She experienced no anger or repulsion in the voice of the One who told her she was living in immorality—the One who spoke truth in love. In our culture, truth is often used to accuse or condemn, but Jesus brought the truth to liberate. John 8:32 reminds us that "the truth sets us free." Do you have a desire to know and experience the truth, or are you more concerned with defending the truth? Are you missing the truth when truth is standing right in front of you? Look down. Look around. Truth is all around you. The bush always burns, and the ground is always sacred.

> If we aren't careful, we judge ourselves by our intentions, but we judge others by their actions.

In our culture, it isn't popular to tell the truth. Perhaps that's why we have such a hard time getting to truth. Nicodemus wanted to know truth, and his actions reflected it. Do our actions reflect the same? Someone once said, "Hollywood does a great job of taking what is fake and making it seem real." The church can make what is real appear to be fake. How? We remain silent when truth should be declared, and we preach louder than we live. If we aren't careful, we judge ourselves by our intentions, but we judge others by their actions. Or as Martin Luther King, Jr., once said, "Our lives begin to end the day we become silent about the things that matter."[4]

Question

It only makes sense that we would have questions about God. Even those who walked with Jesus on this earth didn't fully understand everything He had to say. He spoke in parables, rather than clearly explaining Himself. He didn't leave us with a coherent belief system. He asked questions far more often than He gave commandments.

We assume that years of history and cultural barriers make the Bible difficult for us to understand, but this isn't the case. The Bible was hard to understand even for those who lived it. Daniel 12:8 says, "I heard, but I did not understand." Daniel was right in the middle of hearing the very words to be written in the Bible—he was living the very experience—yet he didn't understand. In Matthew 11:25, Jesus says, "I thank you, Father, Lord of heaven and earth, that you have hidden these things from the wise and understanding and revealed them to little children" (ESV). The source of our misunderstanding isn't our intellect but our hearts. Selfish ambition can taint the truth we're trying to hear.

If you've been going to church your whole life but still have questions—good! If you've given the "Christian" thing a try and you're unimpressed, stick with me. We can be impatient with the journey to something unknown, something new. If you aren't sure what Jesus is all about—fine. If you doubt God loves you or cares about what happens to you, keep reading. God isn't afraid of your questions.

In Luke 19:1–5, Jesus chose to draw close to a man whose life was full of mistakes, who had his own fair share of questions, because He liked what He saw in that man's heart. Zacchaeus, known by those around him as a crooked tax collector, made an effort. He didn't "arrive" when He met Jesus but was willing to enter the conversation. He had questions but refused to use those questions as an excuse. Questions are no threat to God. He's the only One who can give us clear answers.

We find the final reference to Nicodemus in John 19:38–42 after the murder and burial of Jesus. A couple of people showed up to ask Pilate if they could conduct a proper Jewish burial for Jesus' body. One was Joseph of Arimathea and the other was Nicodemus. John says Nicodemus brought "myrrh and aloes, about seventy-five pounds"—the equivalent of about $3,500 today. The custom was to bring about twenty pounds, but Nicodemus didn't hold back. Here we see his faith fully develop and solidify. We see the final indication that he was ready to commit his heart to Jesus. His faith had been a journey.

For those of us worried we haven't "arrived" yet in our faith, be encouraged by Nicodemus' journey from confused Pharisee to devoted Christ-follower. We feel self-condemned when we don't immediately "get it." But we don't need to. Faith is always a process. It was for me, it was for Nicodemus, and it will be for you, too. Jesus washed the feet of those who denied, betrayed, and doubted Him. Why? He understood that faith was a journey— and He wants to be with us on that journey every step of the way.

More often than not, we're making immense progress but because we can't see the kingdom of heaven—because we're expecting one big and final event—we become discouraged. Jesus compared the kingdom to yeast, which takes time to rise. Faith isn't an event but a process, which is always at work, whether we know it or not. The bush is always burning. The ground is always sacred.

CHAPTER EIGHT

Four Sleepless Nights

Do you realize and acknowledge your unworthiness?

There's no situation too awful for Jesus—no obstacle too insurmountable for His love. Jesus made it a habit to become personally involved in awful situations. He saw beyond the awful disease of leprosy and, rather than cower in disgust, touched the untouchable. He interrupted the potential execution of the accused adulteress and brought justice where religion triumphed over grace. No matter how dark a circumstance, Jesus will break into that darkness. He's willing to overcome any barrier, to dig through the rubble, just to bring us home.

On Wednesday, December 7, 1988, at 11:41 local time (07:41 UTC), an earthquake shook the northern region of Armenia (then part of the Soviet Union). Measuring 6.9 on the Richter scale, the earthquake was followed by powerful aftershocks that continued for months. Armenia struggled to recover. By United Nations' estimates, more than 25,000 people were killed, 15,000 more injured, and the physical damage equaled $14.2 billion (USD).[1]

I remember hearing the story of a man who walked his son to school that morning. Just like always, he dropped his son off at the front door. Moments after he arrived home, the earthquake hit. The man waited for the shaking to stop before sprinting back to the school to make sure his son was okay.

As he ran, he noticed crumbled buildings on the sides of the streets; traffic had lurched to a stop. People were stunned. Screams echoed in the streets. The city was in shambles, but he kept running. When he arrived at the school, he was horrified by what he saw. The school was in a heap on the ground. Parents and spectators stood around the periphery, sobbing for their losses. Time stands still and troubles are fleeting when what matters most seems to become a vapor.

Onlookers, police, and medical personnel stared at what used to be the school. It was unsafe to venture beyond the established safety zone. This father, on the other hand, didn't waste any time. Immediately, he started to pick up the stones and concrete of the building—some pieces nearly as big as he was—and moved them to the side. Onlookers couldn't believe their eyes. They couldn't believe this father was strong enough to remove the stones from the pile of rubble, and they couldn't believe anyone would be naive enough to think anyone could still be alive underneath.

People urged him to stop. "You know they're dead. You can't help!" they called after him. Even a policeman encouraged him to stop. But the father kept digging.

Hours passed, then a full day passed. Still, no sign of his son—or any other survivor, for that matter. The father kept digging. He didn't eat, didn't sleep. All he did was dig and dig until finally, out of the depths of the rubble, he heard a small sound. He moved toward the

> No matter where we've come from or what church we go to or how "put together" our life is, without Jesus we're in the pit.

noise and began unearthing right in that area. Within minutes, he revealed a small opening, deep below the surface, where several kids were hiding—including his son.

"Arman!" the father cried, reaching down for his son's hand, "grab my hand!"

A voice answered him, "Father, it's me!" Then, he added these priceless words. "I told the other kids not to worry. I told them if you were alive, you'd save me, and when you saved me, they'd be saved too. Because you promised me, 'No matter what, I'll always be there for you.'"

Sometimes when I tell people my life story—that I've come from drug addiction and encounters with demons, crystal meth, near-death experiences, etc.—they think one of two things. Either, *Wow, I'm so glad I don't have a story as dark as Heath's story*, or *Wow, I wish I had a testimony as interesting as Heath's.* Either way, they're missing the point.

The point is we're *all* down in the pit. We are all buried underneath a weight we cannot possibly lift. It's so easy to lose sight of our place "underneath" sometimes—to lean on our spiritual pedigree or our upbringing or achievements. No matter where we've come from or what church we go to or how "put together" our life is, without Jesus we're in the pit. Jesus is digging through the rubble to get to us, and when He finally breaks through, I pray we respond like the rescued son, Arman: Somehow, deep inside my soul, I always knew You were coming. James 4:5 says this perfectly: ". . . he yearns jealously over the spirit that he has made to dwell in us" (ESV).

A Man of Unclean Lips

The closer we move to Jesus and the more aware we become of the work of heaven all around us, the less likely we are to lose sight of our place in the pit. When we move close to Him, or He moves close to us, and we catch a glimpse of who He really is, there is no denying how unworthy we have always been.

Isaiah—the most quoted prophet in Scripture—lived during the times of Amos, Hosea, and Micah. The year King Uzziah died, the Lord visited Isaiah. Uzziah was a strong leader and an efficient king (2 Chron. 26:1–15). So, if Isaiah was like everyone else in Uzziah's kingdom, he was grieving the loss of this great leader. One of the sources of his comfort was gone. Like the disciples in the boat on the Sea of Galilee, a storm was beginning to rage in Isaiah's life. Would he panic and lose sight of what was true? Or would he maintain his sense of identity?

We read in Isaiah 6:2 that angels appeared before him—each with six wings—and they echoed in unison, "Holy, holy, holy is the LORD Almighty. The earth is full of your glory!" Scripture says that even the buildings shook at the sound of the singing. Holiness is the first thought and mention when in the presence of God.

Isaiah's response is telling: "Woe to me!" he said, "I am ruined! For I am a man of unclean lips, and my eyes have seen the King, the LORD Almighty. Then one of the seraphim flew to me with a burning coal in his hand, which he had taken from the altar with tongs. He touched my mouth with it and said, 'Behold, this has touched your lips; and your iniquity is taken away and your sin is forgiven.'" This prophet, whose mouth frequently spoke about God, was suddenly convicted that his mouth was unclean. The vehicle of his spiritual gift was the source of his conviction. Was he a false prophet? Not at all! Isaiah simply realized in that moment how his hard work and good deeds could never measure up to God's holiness. Author C. S. Lewis said, "The real test of being in the presence of God is that you either forget about yourself altogether or see yourself as a small dirty object."[2]

To fully understand the weight of this passage, you have to remember that Isaiah was the prophet who had a vision about the birth of Jesus and prophesied about it. He also saw Jesus crucified (Isaiah 53) and painted a word picture for all of us to see—a picture that even the gospels don't fully describe. Jesus chose Isaiah to send a message to God's people. Through this encounter with the divine, Isaiah understood more about Jesus than any other Old Testament prophet, yet he had barely scratched the surface in knowing God.

If anyone in the kingdom had clean lips, it was Isaiah. But he knew as well as anyone (as he would write later) that what we call righteousness is like dirty rags when presented to Jesus. When we're exposed to Jesus' majesty, we can't help but recognize just how unclean we really are.

Yet God wasn't afraid of Isaiah's humanity. I love this part of the passage. Isaiah was humbled in the presence of God, and yet God still invited him into the greater story. Isaiah 6:8 tells us that the voice of the Lord was heard asking, "Who will go for us? Who can we send?" In other words, all of heaven has a message to share, and we need a messenger. Just because we are unworthy, God doesn't discount us as His messengers. In fact, to be used by God we must realize how *unworthy* we are.

> To be used by God we must realize how unworthy we are.

Another fascinating part about this passage—and an important one for us to remember—is what Isaiah described: "the train of His robe filled the temple" (6:1). Don't miss the significance of this word choice. I've been told the text literally says, "the train of His robe continuously fills and fills and fills the temple." Why is this significant?

An ancient custom during that time went like this: When two armies went to battle, the winning king would take the jewels from the losing king's crown and sew those jewels into his robe. When a king ran out of space on his robe, more fabric would be added so that more jewels could be sewn onto it. The longer the train of a king's robe, the more valiant he and his army had been in battle.

So as God revealed His holiness to Isaiah and Isaiah cowered in fear, God also invited him to come alongside of heaven and to write his story with a God who is always victorious. In fact, there is no end to God's victory. If He is for us, who can be against us? The train of His robe continuously fills the temple.

> No matter how close to God you are, you can always get closer.

Let me ask you this: Is there a realm of God you're oblivious to? When you read this story, do you wonder if you might be missing something? When you think about the boy whose father reached down into the pit, do you assume that boy is you—or someone else? Are you so worried about saving *others* for Jesus that you've forgotten to let Jesus save *you*? If so, I believe Jesus wants you to open your eyes and your heart as He reveals Himself and His glory to you. He wants to reach down and pull you out of the pit. When a follower of Christ forgets what it's like to be lost, it can be dangerous.

No matter how you answer those questions, God's train keeps filling the temple. No matter how far from God you are, He comes to unbury you from the rubble. No matter how close to God you are, you can always get closer.

Scripture says in Matthew 11:12 that His kingdom is "forcefully advancing and violent people are attacking it" (NLT). Essentially, if we slow down and stop growing in the grace of God, we can actually find ourselves going backward. Life with God isn't about striving to please Him. It's about resting in what Jesus did for us on the cross. Life in Christ gives us each a hot coal, like the one the angel used to cleanse Isaiah's lips, and we decide what to do with it. We can let it sit on the altar of God and slowly burn out. Or, we can fan it into flame (2 Tim. 1:6). We can offer it up and allow the breath of Jesus to turn it into the gift we've been asking for all along.

Home With Jesus

The long-anticipated Wednesday had come—four sleepless nights after my first encounter with Jesus in my room and the night I would go to my friend Gavin's church youth group. I was ready. I knew exactly what I needed to do. I needed to go home with Jesus. I wasn't sure exactly how this worked, but I was sure of one thing. I would show up to youth group that night *without* Jesus and go back home that day *with* Him.

I walked into the small room at the church wearing a Grateful Dead T-shirt. My face was sunken in, and my eyes looked like a raccoon's as I hadn't slept in several days. The black rings around my eyes were telling. I looked completely out of place, yet no one seemed to pay much attention to me. I sat down in one of the chairs that had been set up to form a circle. The small group of students was accompanied by a few adult leaders and there, sitting in their midst, was a police officer. I felt right at home!

It took me a while to figure out what was going on, but eventually I realized the police officer was there to mediate a disagreement between a family in the church who had made death threats against the pastor, and the pastor who was asking this particular family to leave. Conflict, police presence, students crying, dysfunction—this definitely wasn't your average church service. However, I could relate to everything taking place. Jesus wastes nothing! In spite of everything going on around me, I sat there expectantly—ready to do whatever it took to know Jesus.

I had no idea what a "regular" church service was supposed to look like. I just had faith that if I showed up, God would meet me there. That's good theology by the way. James 4:8 says, "Draw near to God, and He will draw near to you." *The Message* puts it this way: "Say a quiet yes to God, and he'll be there in no time."

A few minutes into the service, a volunteer youth leader asked everyone to close their eyes in prayer, so I did. There was no sermon that night. No worship. I'm glad. That gave me less to sift through on my way to encounter Jesus. With the faith of a child, I believed that if I would simply ask Jesus to change my life, He would. I stood up, walked forward about ten feet at the invitation of the preacher, prayed, and in that moment I felt peace. I knew peace.

The prayer I prayed that day—that God would change my life—was answered in an instant. I was set free from drug addictions and the many layers of baggage in my life. My body was healed from the side effects of the life I'd been living. I felt right at home with Jesus. Did all of my troubles immediately vanish? No. Actually, I became more aware of some areas of my life that weren't healthy. We don't submit to Jesus to make our life better. We submit to Him because He is God.

Amazingly, incredibly, miraculously, my life changed that night. This tends to happen when we surrender to God's purpose for our lives and abandon our own. I couldn't help but be mesmerized by Him. Suddenly, my dreams and desires changed; my whole life changed. I didn't have to strive or fight for everything to be different. It just was. I found my attention diverted from schoolwork to Bible reading. I was a great student, so I felt motivated to maintain my GPA, but homework was merely a stepping stone to get to where I truly wanted to be—at home, alone in my room, with Jesus.

I honestly didn't understand much of what I read. I didn't have to at that point. My heart came alive with every word on the page. My heart understood the words, and my mind caught up. I remember reading in Genesis 1 where God spoke the universe into existence. I had studied theories of origin from Hinduism to Neo-Darwinism. It never really struck me as unusual that God spoke and existence began. I didn't need to understand. I was home with Jesus, and when you're home with Jesus, your need to understand all the details takes a back seat to your need to know more about Him. Embracing what we don't fully understand is a privilege in life.

I stayed up that night after meeting Jesus and read the New Testament. I thumbed through Psalms. I came across a book called "Job" and honestly thought there was a book in the Bible about different "jobs" God could give you. At the end of the Bible, in Revelation, I remember reading where the dragon suffered defeat and Jesus won. This was important to me since my encounters with the unseen world made it so much more real. I also remember thinking, *Why is Satan described as a serpent in Genesis but in Revelation he's described as a dragon? Did someone feed him?*

The next morning I drove through McDonald's, ordered a Coke, and then drove around back to the dumpster where I threw away all of the drugs and paraphernalia I had in my car. I went to school, and I was different. Everyone noticed. Not only was I sober—I also was new person. Brand new. Jesus breathes life into dead places. He's the rain in our Death Valley. He's at work, even where we don't see it. Jesus breathed life into me.

A Miraculous Letter

After school that same day, I pulled into my driveway and walked to the mailbox to check the mail. I'm not sure why. I never checked the mail. (Some of you reading this book may be unaware, but mail used to come in the form of paper and was dropped off at your house.) Why I chose to check the mailbox that day is beyond me. But I'm glad I did. Inside the black box with the red flag on the side was a letter written to me from the young girl in the hallway. Her name was Ali.

I opened the letter. She had written page after page of answers to the questions I had asked in eighth grade about Jesus. The answers she wasn't interested in sharing with me then, she shared with me now. She broke the silence. I don't know why the letter showed up that day, but it was perfect timing. God's timing always is. I still had the questions, but now I was asking them from a brand new perspective, thanks to Christ's mercy, and He provided the answers. I wasn't alone in my new relationship with Jesus. Others knew Him as well.

Why Ali held onto the letter for so long before she decided to mail it, neither of us will ever know. Why the letter showed up on that exact day is a mystery left for heaven. Ali had crafted the letter weeks before she sent it. Rather than mailing it right away, something inside her compelled her to wait. Walking through the mall, Ali was compelled to mail it at just the right time. It was the right time, indeed.

Ali and I spoke off and on after that, although we attended different schools. We graduated from high school and started college. Eventually, we were married. God knew all along what He was doing when He whispered quietly in the heart of that young girl in the hallway by her locker: "Pray for him. Someday, he will be your husband. I have a call on his life to preach." We realize now that she had much more than a mere thought in that hallway. She found herself standing on sacred ground and was unaware then.

> What if God is calling out to you right now? The moment may be unannounced, but if you slow down, you can hear it.

Much later, I would find some of those old prayer journals where she meticulously wrote her prayers at 2:53 a.m., "God, I pray that you would reveal yourself to Heath." God did, thanks to Ali who dared to listen when He whispered; thanks to Gavin who dared to invite me to a church service, regardless of how imperfect it was; and thanks to the prayers of Ali and her mom who dared to believe that eternity hinges on the word "if."

If Ali and her mom hadn't prayed, what would the outcome have been? If they hadn't been tuned in to what God was doing all around them, what would they have missed? If they hadn't turned and seen the burning bush, would they have missed it forever? Would I have missed my chance to step into eternity with Jesus? We'll never know for sure what would have taken place. I don't know about you, but I don't want to miss my moment. I don't want to miss what could be my last chance. What if God is calling out to you right now? The moment may be unannounced, but if you slow down, you can hear it.

Did you know God is inviting you into a beautiful piece of artwork? It's true. He's painting a masterpiece, and He wants you to be a part of it. But for it to work, you have to play the role you were designed to play, with the colors you were made to paint. It took me four sleepless nights to step back and look at the masterpiece He was painting.

Paul alludes to the beauty of God's art in one of his writings. In his letter to the church at Ephesus, Paul told them, "You are God's workmanship" (Eph. 2:10). Workmanship is a peculiar word. Originally recorded in Greek, the word used here is poema from which we get our word "poem." I was a poem, and the writer meticulously wove verse upon verse together.

Over time, I became used to the sound of the brush hitting the surface. The colors, although beautiful and unusual in combination, became part of my everyday life. Through the cloak of darkness that had once settled over my life, I finally began to see how colorful God's art was. I finally was able to turn and see—not with physical eyes as much as with spiritual ones—how the bush is always burning and the ground is always sacred.

To me, the most amazing part of the story is this: I wouldn't be where I am today if it weren't for that young girl. If she hadn't responded to the call God put on her life to pray, if she hadn't prayed obediently, if she hadn't written that letter, I might not be sitting at my computer, writing these words. I'm the product of one individual slowing down long enough to listen when God spoke, daring to believe, daring to recognize the potential in Death Valley.

Think about that. The simple act of slowing down long enough to notice and respond changed a stranger's life and rewrote a story. All of creation is waiting, with bated breath, for someone to wake up to the voice of the Spirit and live in that wakeful state. When you wake up, you wake others up. It's a domino effect. The world will look dramatically different when our souls awaken to what God has been doing all along, without our knowing. The bush is burning. The ground where you walk is sacred.

An Encounter With Jesus

If you remember no other part of my story, I pray you remember this: An encounter with Jesus changed everything. If you consider yourself a believer, but you've never had a "profoundly changed" story like I've told here, I challenge you to take a second look at your spiritual life, your spiritual eyes. The very people who murdered God were the ones who were supposed to have known Him the best.

Remember Nicodemus? What I find so fascinating about Nicodemus is that he was profoundly committed to knowing the Lord. He had a committed prayer life—better than my prayer life at times and possibly better than yours. He had numerous parts of the Old Testament memorized. As a committed Jew, he was circumcised, had followed the law down to its tiniest letter, and even carried a net to strain his drink in accordance with the laws of his faith. And yet when he came to Jesus he said to him, "Rabbi, we know you are a teacher from the Lord . . ."

Did you catch that? He said, "Rabbi . . ." Even while acknowledging that Jesus was someone special, he missed it. What he should have said was, "We know you are the Lord." Someone had switched the lid of the puzzle box. Nicodemus was looking in the right place for the wrong thing.

What can we learn from Nicodemus? Maybe that many Christians—many of us—think we know things about Jesus we don't actually know. Just because someone has a religious routine, a rhythm, a position, a title or a circle of influence doesn't mean they are known by God. Religious life has its benefits. It can give you a happier marriage, well-behaved kids, a good job, affluence and success and these things can pose as the fruit of knowing God. But there can be a fine line between being close with Jesus and being simply moral and self-sufficient. We should all be wary of being or becoming the former. This is one of the most grounding, humbling thoughts in my life.

Still, notice how Jesus responded to Nicodemus. He said, "Unless you are born again, you won't be able to see the kingdom." So in other words, while Nicodemus was looking for signs of the Messiah, Jesus said he should be looking for the kingdom. The only way to see the kingdom is to be born again, to be born in the *Spirit*. The only way to see the kingdom is to develop a profound awareness. God is here. He has always been here. If you worry that you don't have eyes to see, ask Him to help you. He always responds.

If you feel like you've been in a dark corner and nobody cares, I understand. I was a companion of darkness myself. If you want to be close to Jesus but feel like you might be far away, I know how you feel and I want you to know: We're always as close to Jesus as we want to be. He is profoundly present. The bush always burns, and the ground is always sacred. If you have doubts about God, I say, "Welcome to the club." I've had doubts. Nicodemus had doubts. But he didn't let his doubts get in the way of ultimately encountering Jesus. In fact, his doubts just may have been what led him home. So were mine. So might yours.

CHAPTER NINE

Don't Act Like a Christian

Are you so caught up with living like a
Christian that you miss meeting Jesus?

I t's easy to forget how far God has brought us. Anytime we become aware of His presence, we are changed. In the presence of love, we understand. Yet it doesn't take long before we begin to forget what it felt like to be lost.

After that night at the strange church service, I was so excited about Jesus I couldn't stop talking about Him. I went home and told my mom how real Jesus had become to me and that I had submitted to His mercy. Some elderly ladies at church baked brownies for me, and I took them to the place where all the homeless people hung out. I passed the brownies around and shared about Jesus and how good He was.

I went to nursing homes to talk about Jesus, visit with the residents, and pray for the sick. I went to the mall and talked about

Jesus. I talked about Him at school, to my friends, to anyone who would listen. My goal wasn't to convert people but to love them, the way I had been loved. Whenever we build relationships to convert someone, it's an indicator of how shallow we've become. I just couldn't keep the good news quiet.

During Sunday services at church, I remember catching some harsh stares from people when I flipped up my middle finger and pointed it downward during worship. My goal was to lift my voice to Jesus and honor Him and send a clear message to the Devil that I was no longer interested. But a person giving the finger to Satan is an awkward sight to someone wearing a choir robe. My heart was in the right place, even if my actions were strange. I wanted everyone to know what Jesus had done in my life. I wanted everyone to see the incredible things that were happening because of Him.

But after a brief moment of knowing Jesus, I began to forget. It's amazing how fast it happens. When I first met Jesus, I felt desperate to be like Him. Before I knew it, I was desperate to be like Christians. I was "lost" again, and I didn't even know it.

King on Earth, Man in Heaven

This tendency to forget reminds me of King Saul. The story of Saul fascinates me because for all intents and purposes, Saul shouldn't have been king. The nation of Israel was considered a theocracy (meaning they were guided by the sovereign God rather than a dictator or elected official). Every other nation and kingdom surrounding the Hebrews was ruled by a king, but the Hebrews were called to do life differently.

In 1 Samuel 7, God miraculously brought relief to Israel during a battle. Then, in the very next chapter, we see the Hebrew people telling Samuel, "Here's what we want you to do: Appoint a king to rule us, just like everybody else" (1 Sam. 8:5–7). When Samuel heard their demand—"Give us a king to rule us!"—he was crushed. How awful! Samuel prayed and God essentially said, "Go ahead and do what they're asking. They're not rejecting you. They've rejected me as their King" (1 Sam. 8:7). So Samuel set out to find a man fit to be king.

> Sometimes the things that seem to take us most profoundly off the path of productivity (like an unexpected encounter with someone) are the things that put us on the path of God's plan.

Samuel found Saul, who wasn't exactly "fit to be king"— at least not from the description of Saul in 1 Samuel 9. One of the first things we learn about Saul is that he was looking for his father's donkeys. This is the level of responsibility his father was willing to give him: recovering livestock. On his search for the missing donkeys, Saul bumped into Samuel who happened to be looking for a king. Sometimes the things that seem to take us most profoundly off the path of productivity (like an unexpected encounter with someone) are the things that put us on the path of God's plan.

First Samuel 10 tells us God touched Saul and changed him into a new person (verse 6). Pay attention to what happened next. Saul was so terrified by what God had called him to do that he hid among the baggage rather than be presented to the people as their king (verse 22). Often, the work God calls us to do is far too big for us to accomplish on our own. We aren't qualified. We shake in our boots. It's comforting to know that Saul felt inadequate to the call on his life. Thank goodness I'm not the only one, nor are you.

But the story doesn't end here. God led Saul into a great military victory and afterward, gave him clear instructions: "Destroy everything. Take nothing for yourself." Instead of obeying, however, and being humbled in the presence of God's mercy, Saul acted in his own strength and kept some of the plunder. Saul had been selected by God to be king, despite his misgivings about himself. Yet in *one* act—*one* desire of his flesh to accomplish his personal ambition in spite of God's instructions— it was over. God removed His hand of favor. If that doesn't cause you to pause, I don't know what will.

From that moment, things shifted in heaven. Saul sat on the throne, but God had essentially removed the kingdom from him. Later, it would be given to an insignificant seventeen-year- old named David (1 Sam. 13:13–14). Meanwhile, Saul led the nation to destruction in his own strength. Why? First Samuel 15:11 says it all. Saul didn't do what God asked him to do. His disobedience and selfish ambitions sabotaged God's purpose and plans for his life.

It's sobering to read how this all wraps up in 1 Samuel 15:17. Scripture tells us that Saul wasn't always this way. There was a time when he was "little in his own eyes," (a reference to hiding among the baggage), yet he became a king whose reputation and image were his primary concern. He went to great lengths to maintain his reputation, to uphold the approval of the people so he wouldn't be replaced as king. But he forgot that the people didn't decide who would be king. God did. The people had never put Saul in his position of leadership. God had.

God can use anybody—literally anybody—to fulfill His purposes. But something dangerous happens when our image and reputation become our primary concern. The favor of heaven can be pulled right out from under us. This can happen easily, not just to those who hold tangible leadership positions, but to all of who follow God. If we use our position and platform for personal gain, if we lean on our own spiritual clout and reputation above God's mercy, if we forget we were once in the pit, if we lose sight of how far God has brought us, our arrogance will destroy not only us—it also will impact an entire kingdom. It happened to Saul, and it can happen to each of us, even committed Christians, if we're not careful.

> May we never allow our public reputation to outweigh our private devotion.

A Monument or a Privilege

I've heard it said, "Don't wait for a spotlight to make you into something. . . . Spotlights only reveal who you already are." Like Saul, we can become image managers. We can become proud. We forget that leaders make the greatest hypocrites because of their ability to persuade and deceive. Rarely is there a pastor or leader whose character exceeds their reputation. Too often, we use the abilities God has given us for our own purposes. Too often, we use our God-given resources to uphold our own image. Too quickly we forget the source of the miracles around us—miracles that happen not by our own strength, but because the bush always burns and the ground is always sacred. May we never allow our public reputation to outweigh our private devotion.

God chose Saul, but Saul didn't finish strong. His humble beginning had all the ingredients for success—if only he had remembered who he was before God stepped in and lifted him up to a position of authority.

Saul was only thirty years of age—far too young and inexperienced to be ruling a kingdom—but God saw his potential. Then Saul took the plunder he was supposed to destroy. Moses murdered an Egyptian. Both men must have found themselves in emotional, mental, and spiritual deserts. Meanwhile, God was trying to get their attention. Moses turned and saw what God was doing. Saul watched as his kingdom, and his purpose in life, slipped through his fingers. The only difference between these two men? Their willingness to see.

First Samuel 16:14 tells us, "the spirit of the LORD had departed from Saul." We know God's Spirit is not afraid of a desert—physical, spiritual, or otherwise. The desert is where the burning bush showed up for Moses. But here we see what can happen when arrogance, pride, and image-management take over. We forget just how desperately we need God. The Spirit of God can depart from us. God felt more welcome in the desert with Moses than He did with Saul. The only difference was Moses' willingness to notice.

At one point in Saul's life, the bush was still burning and the ground was still sacred, but he refused to turn aside and see. It's tragic how hard God tried to get Saul's attention. But Saul was too busy focusing on himself. He lacked identity and didn't understand who he was meant to be. He was building his puzzle with the wrong lid.

Like Saul, my life circumstances were altered in a moment—not because of anything I did but because of what God did *in* me. I started fasting and witnessing miracles. I watched the name of Jesus cast demons out of people on the streets—usually right after I handed them a brownie. But what happened to Saul happened to me in a way, too. I had my moments of forgetting. Saul forgot about God's mercy. And as we read in the book of 1 Samuel, God regretted making him king.

What about us? If we're in a position of leadership—and many of us are, whether or not we would call it that—do we consider how our position of influence has been gifted to us? Do we allow our egos and insecurities to get in the way? Do we consider our position to be a privilege of God or a monument to our own greatness? As believers, are we aware of the depth of God's mercy in our own lives? Have we forgotten the pit we were once in?

Saul is a tragic example of how far we can go and how unthinkable our actions can become when we lose sight of God. Unless we practice the profound awareness of His presence, His mercy is easy to forget—not because His mercy is deficient but because the human heart is found lacking.

Learning to Be a Christian

I had my own moments of forgetting. Within months of knowing Jesus, I was wearing all the right clothes, listening to all the right music, volunteering at church, and going to services several times each week. While there's nothing wrong with these things, for me being a Christian had become more about maintaining an image than being close to Jesus. Knowing Christ brings a strong morality to our lives, but strong morality doesn't always lead us to Jesus. I allowed church busyness and a subculture to rob me of opportunities I could have had with people. If we're not careful, our desire to be like Christians will actually rob us of our desire to be like Jesus.

If you've been a Christian for any length of time, you've probably read or heard the story of the prodigal son (Luke 15). In that story, Jesus described a young man who had done all the right things. He had worn the right clothes, listened to the right music, shown up at church multiple times a week, volunteered in the least desirable positions, had always been the "yes" man—yet, at the end of the story, his heart was far from the father. You might know this man as the "older brother." He lived in his father's house, sat at his father's table, but lost touch with his father's heart.

> When we focus more on Christianity than we do on Jesus, we quench the fire of the Holy Spirit in our lives.

This man's younger brother was also distant from their father but in a much different way. He came to his father and asked for his inheritance early so he could spend it on whatever he wanted. Essentially, he said to his father: "You're dead to me. I'm going to live my life my way." On the outside, this son was rebellious, frivolous, dangerous, and ill-advised, but he was actually the *first* of the two brothers to return to the father. Our need for God draws us back to Him.

If our need for the Father draws us back to Him, and if our need for God can be so easily numbed by our spiritual routine (right clothes, right words, right church attendance), then it makes sense that those of us who have been walking with Jesus for a while might be in the most danger of forgetting our need for Him—of waking up one day and realizing we've drifted far from Him. Even as we've sat at His table, we've been far from Him. Even in His house, we can't see that the bush has always been burning.

Let me be clear. I'm not saying Christianity is irrelevant or church is irrelevant. But if we aren't watchful, the rhythm these things bring to our lives can desensitize our souls. It's so easy. You don't need a dramatic exit. You don't have to be like the young son and ask for your inheritance and storm out. There may not be any major rebellion or misconduct. It can be as simple as bowing a head and quickly rushing through a prayer before a meal, or reading the Bible without letting the Bible read who you are. The Enemy loves this—because the fade can be so silent and subtle that people around you (and even you) don't know it's happening.

To be clear, we don't necessarily lose our salvation when we leave the Father's house so to speak, but we might lose something even more valuable: our sensitivity to the Holy Spirit. We lose intimacy with Jesus. We lose the sense and understanding of being close to Him. Just like a marriage relationship, if we stop communicating and stop seeking to notice each other, we might stay married legally, but we miss the most beautiful part of the marriage—intimacy, friendship, and satisfaction. First Thessalonians 5:19 says, "Do not quench the spirit." When we focus more on Christianity than we do on Jesus, we quench the fire of the Holy Spirit in our lives. We might stay "married" legally, but are we awake to each other?

After just a few months of being a Christian, this is what happened to me. Some things in my life changed because they needed to. I left a few friendships behind. I definitely ditched my destructive habits. But some things changed only because I thought they "should" change. I assumed they needed to change if I was going to be a good Christian. Here's the thing I didn't realize: There's a difference between being a "good Christian" and actually following Christ. Jesus revolutionizes our lives and takes us from spiritual death to spiritual vibrancy. As with the man possessed by Legion, He doesn't simply modify our behavior. He doesn't focus on our issues. He casts out our demons and gives us new life.

The Danger of Forgetting

It was Friday afternoon when I stood near the doorway of Pete's Pizza across from my high school. I had already devoured two slices of pepperoni with extra sauce and a large Mountain Dew (as a teenager, you don't think much about angioplasty or cavities, do you?), and now I was standing there talking casually with a friend. At this point, I had already encountered the Lord, and He had radically changed my life. But this was a friend I had gotten high with countless times in this same parking lot.

I knew he was hungry for truth, like I had been before Truth sought me out. I could see myself in him. So as we stood there in the parking lot, I felt the overwhelming urge to invite him to church—the only way I could think of to help him see what I had seen. Decades have passed since that moment, yet I can still smell the air, see his face, and feel my heart race a little the way it did when I anticipated what I was about to say. I still see his grin when he turned around one last time as he walked away.

"You're coming to church with me on Sunday, alright?" I told him, not giving him much of a choice. "I'll pick you up around 9:30. Cool?"

"People like me don't go to church" he responded.

"People like me don't belong in church either," I assured him. "I'm picking you up at 9:30."

He listed a dozen other excuses: "I don't have any church clothes, man. This weekend won't work. Maybe another time." Then he turned to walk away and yelled over his shoulder, "I'll see you tonight if you go to the party." He knew I wouldn't be at the party. I had stopped drinking and using drugs months ago.

Honestly, I had the urge to stop him, to convince him. Something deep inside me said, "Heath, be bold and go after him." But I hesitated. I wasn't ashamed to invite him. At this point in my life, I was speaking in nursing homes, homeless shelters, on the streets with drug addicts and the homeless, and with wealthy business people downtown. I took every opportunity to share the truth I had found. It wasn't fear that gripped me. Or shame. I was gripped by something I didn't know could grip you until that point—I would call it "tomorrow."

Meanwhile, as my friend walked away, he turned around, made eye contact with me once more, smiled, and walked up the hill until he was out of sight. Little did I know I would never see him again.

Saturday morning, another friend called. "Did you hear what happened?" he asked.

I hadn't, but before I could say no, he began sobbing on the other end of the line. Our friend—the one I'd invited to church only hours earlier—died at the party that night.

I couldn't believe it. The very guy I had eaten pizza with just twelve hours before, the very guy the Holy Spirit had prompted me to "go after" and share the gospel with—was no longer on this earth. It was much more than a gut check on that Saturday morning. It was horrible, sorrowful, and emotionally overwhelming. I blew it. I had missed an opportunity, and so had my friend. What would have happened if I had been bold and gone after him? What would have happened if I hadn't made "tomorrow" my excuse? Maybe my friend wouldn't have missed his last opportunity to hear the truth of Jesus.

> Sometimes the saboteur to eternity isn't fear, shame, or embarrassment but a lack of urgency to the activities of heaven happening all around us.

Years later, I found myself married with children and sharing a meal of homemade tacos in the basement of some family friends. (Homemade tortillas made in a FryDaddy always go well with conversation.) The kids were running around, our wives were talking, and I found myself talking about Jesus. I shared stories from my adolescence—the brutal mistakes I'd made and how God had rescued me. We discussed the lessons we had learned from God as we failed, got back up, and walked on in His love. After some time of sharing, I decided to tell my story of letting "tomorrow" sabotage a moment.

Immediately after I finished my story, he looked at me and said, "You were the one? You were the one who invited him to church that weekend?" I listened while he recounted a conversation he'd had with my friend's brother and mom the day of the funeral. Apparently, my friend had come home from school that day asking his mom if she would go to church with him that Sunday. He said a friend had invited him. Only eternity records what happened in the last moments of my friend's life. But no matter what, God's grace covers us even in places where we can't go. God's grace covered me in that moment, and I know it covered my friend, too.

To my knowledge, no one is certain of his cause of death. But we do know that Solomon was right when he said that God had put eternity in the hearts of men.

If is a small word—only two letters—and all of eternity hinges on these letters. "If only I had . . ." I choose not to let this word haunt me. Now, my answer to Jesus is always yes, long before I even know what He is going to ask. If the dead could speak, I wonder what they would say. I think they would say something about "missed opportunity" and "seizing the moment."

Sometimes the saboteur to eternity isn't fear, shame, or embarrassment but a lack of urgency to the activities of heaven happening all around us. The bush is always burning, and the ground is always sacred.

Truth Is Cultural

If acting like a Christian doesn't indicate that we follow Christ, how should we act? When I say the word *Christian*, what puzzle lid do you see? Scripture is filled with compelling verses to support the ultimate choices God invites us to make. Ephesians 2:10 says we're "created in Christ Jesus to do good works." Romans 12:1 records that our lives are to be "holy and pleasing to God." Our obedience to God in tandem with His Word can catch His attention and please Him. But how do we know for sure that we're following Jesus and not just Christianity?

Second Chronicles 16:9 says, "For the eyes of the LORD range throughout the earth to strengthen those whose hearts are fully committed to Him." The "actions" that glorify our Father in heaven are those that bear much fruit (John 15:8). This fruit is described as, and looks like "the fruit of the Spirit—love, joy, peace, patience, kindness, goodness, faithfulness, gentleness, and self-control" (Gal. 5:22–23). Jesus summed it up in Matthew 5:16, "In the same way, let your light shine before others, that they may see your good deeds and glorify your Father in heaven." Our deeds should be known and seen. If they aren't, we aren't abiding in Him.

The problem is that truth is absolute, but it's also cultural. If you were to go to Europe and interview Christians there, you'd find they have a different understanding of certain passages of Scripture, different ideals, and different hills to die on than Christians in America. The same thing would happen with Christians in South America, Asia, etc. Each of us filters truth through the culture in which we live. The Holy Spirit enables us to filter truth through the culture of heaven.

Even those who lived in Jesus' day filtered truth through their cultural understandings -culture that was impacted not only by that time in history but by their religious upbringing and social class. So when Jesus said, "You've heard it said, but I say to you . . ." He was challenging them: "You've been filtering truth through your culture, but I want you to begin filtering truth through *Me*." Jesus is perfect theology.

That's a difficult idea to present and even more difficult for many Christians to understand, so if you feel resistant to it, you're not alone. Christians in Paul's day also had a difficult time wrapping their heads around this concept—especially those who had grown up Jewish.

In Galatians 2, Paul explained to the church in Galatia that they didn't have to be circumcised to be a Christian. This was horrifying for the Jewish Christians in that community who had grown up in a society where circumcision was not only the norm but a requirement for young Jewish boys. While the Jewish Christians were horrified about the idea of an uncircumcised Christian, I can only imagine how the Gentile Christians felt about the alternative!

In Romans, Paul addressed the laws about unclean foods. For the Jews, certain foods weren't considered "clean." Additionally, strict cleaning and cooking rituals made the food "safe" to eat. To abandon these rituals and laws would have been unheard of for Jewish believers, but Paul said to them: "For some people, it's okay to abide by those regulations. For others, it's not necessary. Your job is to stop looking to the right and the left and to focus on what you need to do to be in right standing with God." Truth is cultural.

You could also think of it this way: Truth and the gospel are fluid. Truth fills whatever container it's placed in without changing its substance or makeup. It means that loving your neighbor is an absolute truth and absolute commandment. However, loving your neighbor in Mississippi may mean changing a flat tire on the highway whereas loving your neighbor in Lithuania may mean opening up your home to a stranger for a meal.

It's so easy to get caught up in what's "right" for Christians to do or not do that we can miss Christ altogether. This is what happened to the frustrated older brother in the story of the prodigal son. It's what happened for me a few months after I became a Christian, and it's what I have watched happen to countless Christians in the past few decades. I can only imagine that the Enemy is clapping his hands in joy watching us waste our energy arguing over "unclean meats" or the equivalent, rather than focus on introducing people to the *person* of Jesus.

When Jesus is presented properly, we don't always have to tell people how to live. He brings the reality of right living with Him. When people encounter Jesus—when they're empowered by the Spirit—their lives will automatically begin to show fruit. If not, the deficiency is not on God's side.

In John 18, just as tension was beginning to ramp up in Jerusalem and the Jewish leaders were getting fed up with

CHAPTER NINE: DON'T ACT LIKE A CHRISTIAN

Jesus, He was turned over to Pilate and questioned. Pilate asked Him a series of questions, starting with, "Are you the king of the Jews?" Jesus responded by asking a question in return— which He so often does. "Is that something you came up with on your own, or did someone tell you that?" Jesus then made a few vague comments about how His kingdom is not of this world and how He was born to testify to truth.

To that, Pilate asked, "What is truth?" And you know what happened next? Jesus didn't respond. A man asked God "What is truth?" but God didn't give a definitive answer.

Sometimes, when we ask God a question wanting a definitive answer, He responds with a question. Other times, He doesn't give an answer. Contrary to popular belief in our postmodern world, this isn't because absolute truth doesn't exist, but rather because truth is not an idea. Truth is a person, and the person who embodies truth is not insecure nor does He have an image to manage. Jesus didn't need to answer Pilate's question about truth because Truth was standing right in front of Pilate.

Truth is not relative, but there is relativism to the gospel once you understand the absolutes. People all over the world ask, "So what does a healthy Christian look like?" I wonder if Jesus would respond with a question of His own: "What do you think it looks like?" Based on what you know about yourself, your context, the Bible, and your understanding of Jesus, what seems like the right thing to do? This isn't license to become your own moral guide (Judg. 17:6). Instead, it's a call to be in an ongoing conversation with the Holy Spirit. It's a call to recognize how silly it is to fight over the "issues" when bushes are burning all around you. John 16:13 says, "But when he, the Spirit of truth, comes, he will guide you into all the truth." His Word is our map, and the Spirit, along with our conscience, is our compass. Culture is what we enjoy along the journey.

The problem most Christians have is that they're trying to fit a square-shaped gospel into a round-shaped hole. But the gospel doesn't have a shape. Jesus doesn't have a shape. The gospel is fluid, and it fills whatever container it's placed into. The bush always burns. The ground is always sacred. Jesus went—and He still goes— where no one else is able or willing to go.

Just because everyone is being circumcised (or wearing a certain T-shirt) doesn't mean you need to do the same thing. Just because everyone is eating meat you consider unclean doesn't mean you need to join them. Stop looking from left to right and just look to the person in front of you, who represents all truth for all people across all cultures. There, you'll find the answer. Truth is not an idea. He's a person.

Just Jesus

It's so easy to forget what it feels like to need Jesus, but we all need Him. We need Him in every corner and in every circumstance of our lives. We need Him to fill the gaps in every relationship, every conflict, and every physical space that feels untouched by His love. When God reaches His hand down into your story, you can't deny His touch. But when was the last time you thanked Him for what He has done?

The Israelites used to lay stones of remembrance. As they journeyed through the mountains or the valleys, they left a mark on the terrain they traveled and in the path of those yet to come. Stones of remembrance are not just for us but for future generations. I often revisit that night I met Jesus. I think about where my life would be had He not reached out to me. When I drive through my hometown, and encounter places where I dishonored Him before I knew Him, gratefulness—not guilt—emerges. His love covers a multitude of sin (1 Peter 4:8).

Have you forgotten what it feels like to be lost? Are you more concerned about your reputation than you are about your heart? Like Saul, does the opinion of the crowd or culture around you influence you more than the grace of God and the honor He deserves? Are you the older brother?

If so, God wants you to open your heart to Him once again. He wants you to remember the mercy He has for you. Bushes are burning all around you. Will you open your eyes to see them?

CHAPTER TEN

Complicating the Simple

Are you experiencing the revelation of God?

To be honest, Jesus is simple. We're the ones who make Him more complicated than He needs to be, especially when it comes to *following* Him. Love isn't supposed to be difficult. Grace is accessible to all.

When I think back over the life I've lived, I see how simple Jesus is. Although many of the things I walked through were fairly complicated, in hindsight I see how Jesus was always in the midst of them. The bush was always burning, and the ground was always sacred. No matter how lost I was, He was always more simple than I made Him out to be. I looked for Him in so many different places before I realized He was—and always had been— right in front of me.

So if that's the case—if Jesus is simple—what keeps us from understanding Him? Why did the disciples, who walked with

Him on a daily basis, have a hard time understanding what He was trying to say to them? Why, when they asked Him questions, did He respond with parables? Why have we fought for decades over theological issues—and why have churches even split over these issues? If Jesus is so simple, why does following Jesus feel so complicated?

Perhaps it's because someone has switched our lids. Or, perhaps, we've switched our own lids. We don't have bad intentions. We're trying to follow Jesus. We're just building off the wrong puzzle. We have all the pieces of the puzzle. We're just looking to the wrong example, so we can't figure out where everything goes.

Consider, for example, how much time we spend trying to explain things Jesus never explained. Most of the time when people asked Him questions, He responded with more questions. Other times Jesus told parables—stories meant to help people understand biblical truths without speaking to the issue directly.

Jesus invested much of His time in teaching us *how* to think rather than *what* to think. Often, He redirected attention *off* the answer to the question and onto something different. Jesus isn't nearly as concerned about answers as we are.

> Grace doesn't provide an excuse to pay less attention to our lives. Grace demands much more from us than the law ever will.

Answers are important to us because getting answers is how we systematize and measure and keep things in check. We need to stick to our service times so the parking lot doesn't get too congested. We need to have strict rules about male-female friendships so nothing immoral happens. The rules help us keep things in order—which isn't bad. However, rules were never intended to be the ideal. They can give us a great reputation or they can appease our conscience, but they don't give us Jesus. A statement like this can be dangerous if you interpret it as a license or opportunity to compromise the preferred life outlined for us in Scripture. Grace doesn't provide an excuse to pay less attention to our lives. Grace demands much more from us than the law ever will.

Think back to the religious leaders of Jesus' day. Those men were more committed to knowing God than anyone else in the world. They dedicated most of their early years to reading and studying. They spent hours each day fulfilling the law, down to its last letter. Yet they were the people who missed God the most profoundly. They were looking for God in all the wrong places. Someone had switched their lids.

The answer, for us, isn't necessarily to abandon all the rules or rituals and routines that make up our spiritual lives. There's a distinct difference between tradition and traditionalism. Rituals, rules, and routines can enhance our lives. The answer is to worship Jesus above the rituals and routines and to develop profound awareness of His presence with us, to tune into what He is doing and sharing with us and how He is moving—and to hold on to who He is above all else.

For this to work, we have a certain amount of unlearning to do. If we've learned to follow Christianity rather than Jesus—if our lid has been switched—we'll have to get our bearings around a new lid. It's like Jesus said in His first sermon: "You've heard it said . . . but I say to you . . ." Sometimes we have to unlearn what we've always known about God in order to learn the things He wants to reveal to us in this moment. It's not that the old things cease to be true. It's that they become secondary in light of the new revelation. All old wineskins used to be new wineskins (Luke 5:33–39). There's a difference between good and great, better and best.

Are you experiencing the revelation of God? Or are you relying on the revelation of others to build your spiritual life?

Shortly after I became a Christian, I was talking with a friend and telling him all the incredible things God was doing. I shared how I was taking brownies downtown, and how I'd watched God cast demons out of people and how my entire body was healing from the effects of drugs and alcohol. He listened to me and then looked at me seriously and said, "Heath, you need to pace yourself. If you don't slow down, you're going to burn out."

His advice could have been construed as wise in the eyes of the world. It's true that if we run too hard and too fast toward something, we might burn out. But you can never run too hard or too fast toward Jesus. And Exodus 3 clearly articulates for us in principle that things don't burn out when God is there. He lights the bush on fire, and it is not consumed.

If you've been a Christian your entire life, you may need to step back and take a look at what you *think* you know about God. Do you need a fresh revelation of who He is? Is your spiritual life more ritual and routine than miracles and movements? Has someone switched your lid? In prayer, with Scripture in hand, God will reveal to you where you are and who you are.

If you're new to God, be aware how easy it is to lose Jesus in the midst of Christianity. It doesn't make Christianity bad. It just means Christianity is a descriptor of our religion and of who we worship; it isn't the goal of our faith. It can happen in a heartbeat. It can catch you off guard. It can come out of nowhere. Remember that even Mary and Joseph lost Jesus on the way home from the temple. They had just participated in a religious routine, and they lost Jesus in the midst of it. Don't ever lose sight of the saving work Jesus did in your life. That's the lid you're building from.

Whoever you are—whether you're new to church or you've always gone, whether you love God or are skeptical of Him, whether you have questions or think you have answers—don't ever forget what it felt like to be lost.

A Profound Awareness

God miraculously saved Moses' life so he could be part of God's sovereign plan. That's what has happened in my life, and I know it's what God wants to do for you as well.

At one time Moses tried to take matters into his own hands. In Acts 7:17–34, we learn that Moses knew he was called by God to deliver the Hebrews from slavery, but he had a hard time listening to God or hearing from His people. Moses felt frustrated by what was happening to them and he became impatient. In Exodus 2 we read how he lost his temper and murdered an Egyptian man. His intentions were good—sort of. But he had completely forgotten to submit to God. He was building from the wrong puzzle lid.

Once someone discovered the murder, a forty-year-old Moses had to flee into the desert to hide. He thought that hiding out would save him—as many of us do—but whatever we bury in the sand will one day be resurrected. Only what is covered by the sacrifice of Jesus remains unknown in eternity.

Surely Moses heard the story of God's promise to Abraham in Genesis 12. He knew the end of the story, but his circumstances didn't align with God's promises. Have you been there? Have you ever felt like you understood God's promises completely only to arrive at your destination and feel like nothing had gone the way you wanted? At that moment on Mount Horeb (which in Hebrew means "waste"), God spoke. Sometimes God has something to share with us when we arrive at a destination we didn't foresee.

> We must learn to embrace the promises of God when our circumstances seem to be diametrically opposed to what Scripture teaches.

God only spoke after Moses turned aside to "see" the burning bush: "Take the shoes off of your feet; the place you are standing on is holy." The ground is always sacred. The bush is always burning. Moses had to be willing to see what had been happening all along. No place is void of God's presence. The ground is sacred because it is the presence of the One who fills the earth.

When Moses experienced God's presence in the burning bush he became an answer to the cries of God's people in Egypt. Before, he couldn't hear or see, but now he could. Is it possible God takes us into the desert to provide an opportunity for us to turn aside and hear His voice? When we hear the voice of God, we can become the answer to someone's prayers. That's what happened for Moses, simply because he noticed what many others had overlooked.

Somehow, we must learn to hear what God is saying in the midst of circumstances. Conversations are happening in heaven right now, and your name is spoken by the lips of the One who spoke the world into existence, who spoke audibly to Moses. Even when those circumstances appear to be in contradiction with His Promises—He is among us.

Sometimes, the problem isn't our circumstances but our perception of the circumstances. Remember, Judas and Jesus stood on the exact same ground. They shared the exact same experiences. But the outcomes of their lives were remarkably different.

We don't believe because we understand. We understand because we believe. As Christ-followers, we must learn to embrace paradox and the fact that God answers prayer by silence as much as He answers prayer with a miracle. We must learn to embrace the promises of God when our circumstances seem to be diametrically opposed to what Scripture teaches. Why? Because His ways are not our ways. Sometimes, He's up to something, and we're not aware. A bush can be aflame, and we may not notice it.

Disenfranchised

I know some of you who are reading this book feel angry at Christians and at church. You're no stranger to the church world. You've grown up around Christians. But you've seen the hypocrisy firsthand. Sometimes hypocrisy can prevent us from

THE BUSH ALWAYS BURNS

seeing the goodness of Jesus. This is just another way our lids get switched. When anything other than Jesus becomes our dominant fixation, we lose sight of what really matters. When we are not profoundly aware of Him, we fix our eyes on other things.

I understand this, too.

Shortly after I became a Christian, a leadership transition took place at the church I had been attending. As is often true during transitions, people and situations needed extra attention. Some things were ignored for a long time that needed to be addressed. When the new leader began his position, we all hoped he would take care of things—but this wasn't necessarily the case.

To make matters worse, at one point the leader called my house and asked me to come in one Sunday morning before church. He asked me to stand up on the platform that morning and tell the entire congregation how much I believed in his leadership. As a young believer, I wasn't sure what to do. I was still naive and thought everyone who attended church lived according to Scripture and always treated one another with kindness. I was oblivious to the fact that church wasn't always peaceful. I didn't feel comfortable standing on a platform, speaking into a scenario I didn't understand. But I also didn't feel like I had much of an option to say no. I decided to say no nonetheless.

Over the course of the next year or so, I watched how irresponsible and arrogant behavior, along with selfish ambition, can destroy the church. It's not *our* church by the way. The church belongs to Jesus.

Nevertheless, it was precisely the hypocrisy I saw in this circumstance as a new believer in Christ that made me feel frustrated about church. I would come to church on Sunday and think to myself, *What I read in the Scriptures is not what I see lived out in real life.* It was incredibly frustrating. I wondered what was wrong with me. I felt the tension of conforming to what Scripture said was supposed to be normal compared with what my experience revealed was normal.

I've since overcome that frustration, but at the time I wanted to walk away from God because of the actions of other Christians. It's amazing how we can blame God for what people do. This was my mistake. By God's grace, I never walked away. We have to learn how to separate who God is from how the people who claim to follow Him sometimes reflect Him.

I'm convinced that most people don't reject Jesus. They reject the brand of Jesus we present to them.

Leaving church because of other Christians can complicate the simple. God didn't call us to "fix" Christians. He called us to follow Him, love Him, love people, and abide in Him to produce fruit that remains.

Broken Promises

If you're reading this and thinking to yourself, *It's actually not Christians I'm mad at. It's God Himself,* I can understand that too. Maybe you lost someone you loved or you felt God had promised you something and it never happened—at least not in the way you anticipated. Now, you have questions for Him. Where was He when you were hurting? Why was your marriage fractured, and how could God just sit by and watch? As a child you may have been abused or your parents divorced and you wonder why

God allowed it to happen. You may not understand why what's taking place in the world seems to go unnoticed by Him.

Where is God when those eight-year-old girls stand on the streets as victims of human trafficking? How do I really know if the Bible is true? How in the world did I end up here in my circumstance and my faith? How did I allow my love for Him to slowly fade away? Where is Jesus, and how can I encounter Him? If this is your story, I don't have all the answers you need, but I hope I can offer at least a little bit of clarity. The bush always burns and the ground is always sacred.

What's preventing you from seeing the burning bushes around you?

In John 7:1–2, the Lord's family asked Jesus if He would be traveling with them to the Festival of the Tabernacles. Ironically, even His own family didn't understand what Jesus spent three and a half years communicating. Proximity doesn't always equal intimacy. Jesus answered no—obeying the leading of the Holy Spirit in a moment that didn't make sense. Of course, this confused His family. They said to themselves (and to Jesus): "If you're trying to build a name for yourself, it only makes sense you should put yourself out there! Already, people doubt you." They didn't understand that Jesus didn't come to make a name for Himself. He came to seek and to save those who were lost.

Jesus' response is telling. He said, "My time has not yet fully come." In that moment, He was so in tune with the Spirit of God that He knew exactly what He was supposed to do—and not do. His family and the disciples didn't understand, but He did.

Sometimes, when it comes to unanswered prayers or lost promises, God's perfect time simply has not arrived.

Ecclesiastes 3:1 says, "There is a time for everything, and a season for every activity under the heavens."

Times and seasons have different durations and different indicators. And although those moments, times, and seasons can be incredibly painful, they are also an invitation into deeper intimacy with Jesus. These are the moments to develop the profound awareness I've talked about throughout this book. Jesus is near. He is always near. The question is, are we aware of Him?

There's no better story to demonstrate the power of timing than Abraham and Sarah. Abraham encountered the divine in an unlikely place and at an unlikely time in life—at the age of seventy-five, the point when, for most of us,

> Sometimes, when it comes to unanswered prayers or lost promises, God's perfect time simply has not arrived.

life would be winding down. God made a promise to Abraham and the promise went like this: He would have a son, and through that son, all of the families of the earth would be blessed. Eventually, all the nations would be blessed as well. So Abraham and his wife, Sarah, being obedient to God, set off on a journey without knowing the destination.

There's so much happening here, culturally and historically. First, having a son was a great honor for any family—not just for Abraham and Sarah. It was the way the family name was passed forward and a legacy could continue. To have a son was to be blessed by God. Additionally, since we know the end of the story, we can see how this story is a precursor to the birth of Jesus—

who would come from the line of Abraham. Abraham wouldn't have known this, but we do. Our ability to trust God's timing has so much to do with our perspective.

Decades passed as God's promise became elusive. Abraham's circumstances didn't line up with that promise—or so it seemed. In Genesis 18:10–15, the Lord appeared to Abraham and declared that within a year, he and Sarah would have a son. When Sarah heard what the Lord said, she laughed and doubted. The Lord responded, "Is anything too hard for the LORD?" Even in the face of Sarah's doubt, God reaffirmed His promise to the elderly couple.

At the age of one hundred, Abraham had a son, Isaac. Sarah, by the way, was ninety when she gave birth to this child. If I were God, this isn't the way I would have done it. I would have had Sarah conceive when she was much younger, stronger, and better prepared to care for a young baby. But God's timing is never our timing. His ways are not our ways. And no matter how much we doubt His presence or His hand at work, no matter how hopeless our circumstances seem, the bush is always burning and the ground is always sacred.

To me, the most fascinating part of this series of events is the way Hebrews 11:11 recounts the story of Abraham and Sarah. Genesis makes it clear: Sarah laughed at God, lied to God, and denied that what He had promised was possible. But the author of Hebrews tells us, "By faith Sarah herself received power to conceive, even when she was past the age, since she considered him faithful who had promised."

So what can we make of this passage in Hebrews? Is it a contradiction? Not at all! It demonstrates the power of grace.

The blood of Jesus is so powerful and the grace it provides so complete, that even if your disobedience is recorded in Scripture, God can forget about it. God not only forgives our sin through Christ, He rewrites our story. He never stops working in our lives, never stops speaking to us, and never ceases to be an active, breathing presence in our midst. The bush always burns and the ground is always sacred.

Remember, when Jesus told His family He wouldn't be attending the festival? Well, a few verses later, after they had already left, Jesus decided to join them. It seems sort of strange when you first read it. His family asked Jesus to join them. He said, "No—it's not my time." They were confused, but He stood His ground. Then, a few verses later, Jesus left for the festival on His own. Was He trying to trick them? Was He lying to them?

No, He couldn't do that. In Numbers 23:19, we read that "God is not man, that He should lie" (ESV). He doesn't play games with us. Jesus was so in tune with the move of the Spirit that He knew exactly where He was supposed to go and when. John 5:30 says, "By myself, I can do nothing; I judge only as I hear. and my judgment is just, for I seek not to please myself but him who sent me." The Spirit can close a door one minute and open it the next. The more we're in tune with the Spirit of God, the more we, too, will be able to see how He's working even in the midst of uncertainty.

The second thing that can hinder us from *seeing* God is that our timeline to see His promises fulfilled is too short. In Scripture, some of God's promises weren't fulfilled for decades, as was the case with Moses who heard the voice of God after forty years of wandering in the desert. Yet he heard the voice at the right time. Other promises weren't fulfilled for several lifetimes. God's promises to one person weren't fulfilled until after that person left the planet. An example of this is the promise God made Abraham in Genesis 12—that He would make his descendants as numerous as the stars. Abraham died without receiving the promise. That doesn't mean the promise wasn't answered. God defines "slowness" differently than we do.

It just might be that a promise God has given you will be fulfilled in your children, or your grandchildren. God's ways are not our ways. Give your faith room to grow big enough to include an answer to prayer you haven't considered yet.

Many of us are simply building from the wrong lid. I know I've been building from the wrong lid on many occasions in my life. It's easy to get stuck in this trap. We have to constantly evaluate what we're counting on to help us understand God. What we think is right is not necessarily right. If you're building from the wrong lid, it's no wonder you're disappointed in God. You're expecting Him to be different than He really is. Isaiah 55:8 says, "'For my thoughts are not your thoughts, neither are your ways my ways,' declares the LORD."

Come Alive

Do you know what I want for you? I want you to come alive in Christ. Most people would say they want this for themselves too, but do they really? Coming alive in Christ—just like coming into this world for the first time—can be incredibly disorienting and painful. It can be difficult and frustrating. Most pastors would tell you that coming to know Jesus will open your heart to joy and peace like you've never known—and they would be right—but coming alive in Christ is also painful and difficult.

Dead people don't feel pain. When you come alive in Christ you suddenly feel all the pain and disappointment you've been holding off your entire life. Even Jesus Himself is not described as a man of much joy. He's described as a "man of many sorrows," (Isa. 53:3), and yet we know that He radiated so much joy and love that children flocked to Him and crowds pressed in against Him. He understood, like Moses did, that the bush always burns and the ground is always sacred.

This whole thing is so much easier than we make it. I'm the product of one person who slowed down long enough to engage me in conversation; one person who was listening closely enough to know how to pray; and one person who was willing to take a chance on Jesus—and then a chance on me. It's just that simple.

A few years ago, Ali and I celebrated our wedding anniversary with our two daughters and had an experience we'll never forget. Since we were married in December, it was only natural to purchase tickets to *The Nutcracker* ballet, get dressed up, and carry our two toddlers out on the town for an incredible night. We pushed through the fog from our breath as we walked through freezing air from our car to the convention center. It was a state-of-the-art facility.

From the beginning, the lights and sounds captivated our little girls. Parents pay money just to stare at their children smiling and laughing at events like this. Our oldest daughter leaned over to Ali and I overheard her say, "Oh Mommy, the Sugar Plum Fairy is so beautiful." Moments later, our youngest daughter, at this time too young for preschool, said, "That man is wearing tights!" The ambiance was perfect, and intermission provided a much-needed break to stretch and grab some water.

After the intermission, the extravaganza of art began again. Our oldest looked at Ali and whispered, "Oh Momma, when I grow up I want to be like the Sugar Plum Fairy." Our youngest, however, at just the right moment when the audience was silent and the music faded, loudly declared to us and everyone who could hear around us: "Gross, his tights are stuck in his bottom!" The innocence of our little girl who became distracted by a man wearing tights, seemingly uncomfortable, was both funny and embarrassing. At the conclusion of the ballet, we left with smiling faces and full hearts.

The ballet was a dream come true for my girls, and Ali and I were elated. It was a great anniversary present for us all.

We scooped up our girls and walked quickly to the car. It was a bitter and cold winter night in Iowa. We strapped the girls in their car seats and tried to stay warm as the car heated up. That's when we heard the sound any parent is familiar with— the sound of a child throwing up in the back seat. We turned around and saw that the reservoir had opened up and flooded our car. We attended to our little girl before attempting to clean up the mess. I dry-heaved as I tried to scoop up the vomit with paper towels. Ali was a super-mom, as always. We cleaned up the mess as best as we could and drove home.

Our hearts were still full, and we were all smiling—the car just smelled.

The next day we went over *The Nutcracker* experience with our girls, as is our custom. We like to share memories and talk with one another. Our oldest daughter summed up her experience by stating how much she loved the Sugar Plum Fairy. Our youngest daughter laughed at the male ballet dancer whose tights seemed unnatural to her and recounted her moment of vomit. To one daughter, the experience entailed future goals, while the other was grossed out and puked. Same experience. Different perspectives.

Regardless of our experience, we're all sharing the same moment. Like Moses, we find ourselves wandering in a space unfamiliar to us—the unannounced moments of life. Regardless of the landscape we see, or more importantly, the landscape we perceive, the realities of heaven are all around us. We just need to identify those times in our lives to slow down long enough to notice and look closely and listen intentionally. When we do, we'll encounter the divine and become an answer to someone's prayer. The bush always burns, and the ground is always sacred.

Endnotes

INTRODUCTION

1. W. A. Criswell, "In a Flame of Fire" (sermon), *The W. A. Criswell Sermon Library*, November 16, 1958, http://www.wacriswell.org/PrintTranscript.cfm/SID/635.cfm

2. Ibid.

3. Ibid.

4. H. Richard Niebuhr, quoted in Philip Yancey, *What's So Amazing About Grace?* (Grand Rapids, MI: Zondervan, 1997), 13.

CHAPTER ONE

1. Albert Einstein, quoted in Anslie H. Abraham, *Why Evil Rules—if God is... A Question of Believers and Non-Believers Alike*, (Bloomington, IN: Xlibris Corporation, 2011), 9.

CHAPTER FOUR

1. Sir Ken Robinson, "How to Escape Education's
   Death Valley" (TED Talk), May 15, 2013.http://
   www.ted.com/talks/ken_robinson_how_to_
   escape_education_s_death_valley?language=en

CHAPTER FIVE

1. C. S. Lewis, *Mere Christianity* (New York:
   HarperOne, 2000), 49.

2. John Piper, "Judas Iscariot, the Suicide of Satan,
   and the Salvation of the World" (sermon), *Desiring
   God*, October 7, 2007. http://www.desiringgod.org/
   sermons/judas-iscariot-the-suicide-of-satan-and-
   the-salvation-of-the-world.

CHAPTER SIX

1. Steve Hill popularized this saying, actually
   attributed to Leonard Ravenhill, during the
   Brownsville Revival. Renee DeLoriae, *Portal in
   Pensacola: The Real Thing Comes Hits Brownsville*
   (Shippensburg, PA: Destiny Image Publishers,
   1997), 7.

CHAPTER SEVEN

1. Henri Nouwen, *Henri's Mantle: 100 Meditations on Nouwen's Legacy*, ed. Chris Glaser (Cleveland, OH: Pilgrim Press, 2002), 87.

2. Ester Buchholz, quoted in Dinah Sanders, *Discardia: More Life, Less Stuff* (Dinah Sanders, 2011), 162.

3. Joyce Meyer, "The Cause and Cure of Worry," (article), *Joyce Meyer Ministries* http://www.joycemeyer.org/articles/ea.aspx?article=the_cause_and_cure_for_worry.

4. Martin Luther King, Jr., quoted in Marty Meehan and Paul Epstein, "Making Noise About Global Warming" (Op-Ed), *The Boston Globe* (December 21, 2006).

CHAPTER EIGHT

1. "Disaster in Armenia, 1988," *Making the History of 1989*, Item #172, http://chnm.gmu.edu/1989/items/show/172 (accessed November 22 2014, 9:20 am).

2. *Mere Christianity*, 126.

Acknowledgements

To God, being infinitely great, who is as high above kings as He is beggars (Edwards), who stooped to breathe life into my dead soul. I'm thankful for your mercy.

To Ali, for slowing down long enough to notice, and for rewriting the story for generations to come with me and Jesus. I cherish you and thank you for allowing me to walk with you on His path.

To Leighton and Dallon, you are cherished by God and adored by Mom and Dad. This life is ours together. May the Lord bless you and keep you. May you always dream the dreams of queens.

To Nana, who dared to believe that He is who He says He is. We love you.

Thank you to Sol and Wini Arledge for seeing His story in our life. Thank you to Steve and Susan Blount for publishing His story. Thank you to Darrell and Ally Vesterfelt, and Lindy Lowry for crafting His story revealed in these pages. And thank you to Ted Dekker for the conversation, confidence, and friendship.

To the dozens at My Healthy Church, the National Leadership and Resource Center, and others along the way, may He receive honor for your investment.

I'm grateful for the unannounced moments in life we will all steward. My prayer is that we would slow down long enough to notice that the bush always burns and the ground is always sacred.

About the Author

A t the age of seventeen, Heath's life was dramatically transformed by an encounter with Jesus. Steeped in drug abuse and the occult, he came to believe in Christ for salvation.

Heath's dramatic salvation experience has led him to serve in multiple leadership roles with global influence. He is intrinsically involved with the World Evangelical Alliance Youth Commission and chairs Empowered 21's Next Generation Network, in addition to serving as a national leader for a ministry serving more than half a million students.

He holds an MA in leadership from Evangel University and is a PhD candidate in religious studies at Chester University. Heath and his wife, Ali, and two daughters currently reside in Springfield, Missouri. Together they endeavor to leave a legacy for generations to come.